HOLY HILARITY

HOLY HILARITY

Inspirational Wit and Cartoons

Cal and Rose Samra

WATERBROOK
PRESS

HOLY HILARITY
PUBLISHED BY WATERBROOK PRESS
5446 North Academy Boulevard, Suite 200
Colorado Springs, Colorado 80918
A division of Random House, Inc.

ISBN 1-57856-281-3

For information about membership in the Fellowship of Merry Christians,
including a subscription to *The Joyful Noiseletter,* please call toll-free 1-800-877-2757,
or write to Fellowship of Merry Christians, P.O. Box 895, Portage, MI 49081-0895.
FMC's catalog offers a variety of prints and Christian humor resources.
E-mail: JoyfulNZ@aol.com. Visit FMC's Web site: http://www.joyfulnoiseletter.com.

Library of Congress Cataloging-in-Publication Data
Holy hilarity : a book of inspirational humor and cartoons / [compiled by] Cal and
   Rose Samra. — 1st ed.
      p.   cm.
   Includes indexes.
   ISBN 1-57856-281-3
    1. Christian life Humor. 2. Christianity Humor. 3. Church Humor.
  I. Samra, Cal. II. Samra, Rose.
  PN6231.C35H65   1999
  230'.002'07—dc21   99-33695
                                                    CIP

Printed in the United States of America
1999—First Edition

10 9 8 7 6 5 4 3 2 1

To all the members of

the Fellowship of Merry Christians,

on earth and in heaven,

who share with us

so much joy, humor, and love.

ⓖ

Contents

Be joyful in the Lord, and merry.

— ST. FRANCIS OF ASSISI

Whence comes this idea that if what we are doing is fun,

it can't be God's will? The God who made giraffes,

a baby's fingernails, a puppy's tail, a crooknecked squash,

the bobwhite's call, and a young girl's giggle

has a sense of humor. Make no mistake about that.

— CATHERINE MARSHALL

Introduction

Our first two books of inspirational humor and cartoons, *Holy Humor* and *More Holy Humor,* were so well received (nearly a half-million books sold in 1997 when they were published) that many folks asked us for more. This book, *Holy Hilarity,* and our fourth book, *More Holy Hilarity,* are the sequels.

This is another collection of our favorite jokes, anecdotes, church-bulletin bloopers, out-of-the-mouths-of-babes quotes, and cartoons from *The Joyful Noiseletter,* the award-winning newsletter of the Fellowship of Merry Christians.

The Fellowship of Merry Christians (FMC) was organized in 1985 by a group of Christian humorists, comedians, cartoonists, clowns, clergy, and health professionals of all denominations who wanted to bring more healing humor and laughter into the lives of churches and families.

Through the years, thousands of FMC members have contributed jokes, stories, and their favorite uplifting Scripture passages to *The Joyful Noiseletter;* many of the Christian world's best cartoonists have contributed material as well.

These FMC members have mined a treasury of timeless Christian joy and humor, some of it from the most unlikely places, even the early years of Christianity. They have discovered that humor, like love, crosses denominational lines. These archives disprove the notion that Christians are relentlessly dour, melancholy, humorless, and joyless, though some individuals might fit that description.

The Joyful Noiseletter is a voice laughing in the wilderness. FMC's ministry is to cheer and encourage people. We are thankful that thousands of pastors of all denominations have used the materials in our newsletter to brighten their sermons and to challenge, cheer up, and wake up their congregations.

We believe it is possible to be reverent, relevant, and moral—and still have fun. We also believe that humor is an important healing tool and that Jesus is a joyful Spirit who used humor in His healing ministry.

FMC member Bob White recently e-mailed us these interesting facts: In 1930, adults laughed an average of nineteen minutes a day, but by 1980, adults laughed only an average of six minutes a day. Yet children laugh up to four hundred times a day. White observed that people seem to be losing the art of laughter and that this could be having a serious effect on their health.

Life deals all of us severe blows that cause grief or sadness. This book, ironically, was put together under very difficult and painful circumstances for us. Rose's beloved mother, Marguerite, died after months of battling an insidious form of cancer. And Cal broke his ankle and hobbled around on crutches for a time. In all honesty, we were not in the mood to compile this book when we started. But as we worked on it, we found our laughter helped the healing process. We hope and pray that *Holy Hilarity* will also have a beneficial effect on your health and state of mind.

We are most grateful to all of the FMC members who contributed to this book. Although we wish we had the space to acknowledge all of you, you'll find acknowledgments for larger contributions on the following pages.

God bless and smile on you all!

For information about the Fellowship of Merry Christians, *The Joyful Noiseletter,* and the FMC catalog of clean-humor resources, call toll-free 1-800-877-2757.

Enjoy!

—CAL AND ROSE SAMRA, editors

1

The Lord's Laughter

ⓖ

A merry heart doeth good like a medicine:
but a broken spirit drieth the bones.

—PROVERBS 17:22, KJV

"People *love* the Bigfoot of myth. Do you
want to destroy it by revealing that I'm just
a hairy hermit trying to find God?"

© Ed Sullivan

One of our church deacons, a barber, at the Baptist church in
Auburn, Alabama, was feeling guilty because he had never wit-
nessed for the Lord. One day a man came into his barbershop
and asked for a shave.

The barber put him in a chair and lathered his face. He thought this would be the perfect time to witness to the customer. Nervously, he asked, "S-S-Sir, are you r-r-ready to m-m-meet the L-L-Lord?"

The man opened his eyes wide, and saw the barber holding the razor with a shaking hand. He jumped out of his chair and took off running down the street with the hair cloth flapping in the wind.

—Lee Swope, Auburn, Alabama

Evelyn Briscoe of Okmulgee, Oklahoma, went to the First Presbyterian Church in Sapulpa, Oklahoma, to hear author Charlie Shedd preach. Mrs. Briscoe heard Shedd tell this story:

A college drama group presented a play during which one character stands on a trapdoor and announces, "I descend into hell!" A stagehand below would then pull a rope, the trapdoor would open, and the character would plunge through. The play was well-received.

When the actor playing the part became ill, another actor who was quite overweight took his place. When the new actor announced, "I descend into hell!" the stagehand pulled the rope, and the actor began his plunge, but became hopelessly stuck. No amount of tugging on the rope could make him descend.

One student in the balcony jumped up and yelled: "Hallelujah! Hell is full!"

A local bishop was the speaker at a banquet for single women and widows. There were more than 150 women there. The centerpieces on the tables were given to the women who had a number on the back of their chairs.

The bishop expressed his regrets that not everyone got to take something home, so he told each of the women to pick a number between 1 and 150 because there are 150 chapters in Psalms. Then everyone would have something to take home.

One older woman, not understanding that they were to keep the numbers to themselves, called out No. 56.

The bishop said he would read the psalm to the group. The first verse:

"Be merciful to me, O God, for men hotly pursue me; all day long they press their attack!"

—VIA IDA MAE GEHMAN, PALMYRA, PENNSYLVANIA

After a worship service at First Baptist Church in New Castle, Kentucky, a mother with a fidgety seven-year-old boy told Pastor Dave Charlton how she finally got her son to sit still and be quiet. About halfway through the sermon, she leaned over and whispered: "If you don't be quiet, Pastor Charlton is going to lose his place and will have to start his sermon all over again!" It worked.

—VIA PASTOR DAVE CHARLTON, NEW CASTLE, KENTUCKY

The *Tennessean* of Nashville sponsored a limerick contest. One of the winners was submitted by Georgia Byers:

Our preacher, the Reverend Grundy,

Baptized my sister last Sunday;

But he lost his grip

And she turned to flip—

She's expected to surface next Monday.

Bob Horner, a postal worker, submitted this limerick about baby boomers:

As Boomers, we once loudly vented

On evils that should be repented.

But as years have gone by,

We cannot deny

We became all the things we lamented.

—VIA GEORGE GOLDTRAP, ORMOND-BY-THE-SEA, FLORIDA

Bruce Burnside of Rockville, Maryland, passed on this limerick which he found in a 1974 bulletin of St. John's Episcopal Church, Georgetown, in Washington, D.C.:

A meticulous postman named Hale

Swam into the mouth of a whale.

He looked all about,

Crying, "Jonah, come out!

Two cents postage is due on your mail!"

Laugh and be merry:

Remember, in olden time,

God made Heaven and Earth for joy,

He took in a rhyme, made them,

And filled them full

With the strong red wine of his mirth.

The splendid joy of the stars:

The joy of the earth.

—JOHN MASEFIELD

"I don't think it's Scotty beaming us up this time."

© Dik LaPine

Asked about his position on whiskey, a Congressman replied: "If you mean the demon drink that poisons the mind, pollutes the body, desecrates family life, and inflames sinners, then I'm against it.

"But," he added, "if you mean the elixir of Christmas cheer, the shield against winter chill, the taxable potion that puts needed funds into public coffers to comfort little crippled children, then I'm for it.

"This is my position, and I will not compromise!"

—VIA REV. KARL KRAFT, MANTUA, NEW JERSEY

You can always identify the pastor of any parish. He's the one who goes around and turns out the lights. Two young priests were discussing how penurious their senior pastor was. Said one: "When he dies, if he sees a light at the end of the tunnel, he'll put it out."

—MSGR. CHARLES DOLLEN, *THE PRIEST*

EPISCOPAL AEROBICS RITE II

Stand

Sit

Stand

Sit

Stand

Sit Still

Stand

Kneel

Stand and Hug

Sit or Stand

Stand or Kneel

Walk

Sit, Stand, or Kneel

Stand

Kneel

Stand

Walk

Shake (hands)

—CHURCH OF THE REDEEMER, MIDLOTHIAN, VIRGINIA, *THE ANGLICAN DIGEST*

Committee: a group of people who individually can do nothing, but collectively can decide that nothing can be done.

—VIA JIM GIBSON, NASHVILLE, TENNESSEE

Aim at the cheerfulness of faith.

—JOHN WESLEY

A pastor, disappointed that things were not "happening" in his church, asked a deacon, "What's wrong with our church? Is it ignorance or apathy?"

The deacon replied, "I don't know and I don't care!"

—REV. STUART A. SCHLEGEL,
SANTA CRUZ, CALIFORNIA

"Your altar call made my client feel like a victim. See you in court."

© Steve Phelps

Cheerfulness and contentment are great beautifiers and are great preservers of youthful looks.

—CHARLES DICKENS

HONK IF YOU LOVE JESUS!

A new teacher who is a devout Christian has a bumper sticker that says "Honk If You Love Jesus!" on the rear of her car. She was driving home one day when she stopped for a red light at an intersection.

While she was waiting, she closed her eyes and said a prayer thanking God for all His blessings. The car directly behind her started to honk.

Still in prayer, the woman said to herself, "Isn't it nice that he loves Jesus!" Then several more cars started to honk too. "What a great witness—all these Christians behind me!" she thought.

She looked in her rearview mirror, and saw the man in the car behind her getting out of his car. "He probably wants to share his faith with me," she said to herself.

Then she noticed that the light was green, so she stepped on the gas and drove through the intersection just before the light turned red.

In the rearview mirror, she saw the assembled faithful she had left behind. "The man who was in the car behind me was waving enthusiastically," she excitedly told her husband when she got home. "And all the other people who had been honking had opened their windows and also were waving enthusiastically.

Some were giving the Hawaiian good-luck sign. My students told me it was the Hawaiian good-luck sign."

—VIA DR. JOHN A. DALLES, WEKIVA PRESBYTERIAN
CHURCH, LONGWOOD, FLORIDA

When I was a child, my father was the pastor at Grace Lutheran Church in Rankin, Illinois. At one time he gave his sermon in Swedish at the first service and English at the second service.

On Sunday he would leave early, and the job of getting five children to church on time was left to my mother and older sister. On one winter Sunday morning, colder than usual, we heard the order to be sure our shoes were shined.

There was no time for shoe shining, so we grabbed the next best thing we could find for the job. It happened to be a large jar of Vicks VapoRub. We rubbed it on our shoes to a pretty good shine.

The steam radiators in church were at their best that morning, and we cleared the heads of all the people in the pews.

—AL KARLSTROM, CHAMPAIGN, ILLINOIS

Three children were overheard bragging about their fathers. An investment counselor's son said, "My father makes $60 an hour just sitting at his desk."

"A lawyer's son replied, "My dad talks on the phone for 30 minutes and makes $125."

The pastor's son laughed, "That's nothing! My father preaches for 15 minutes, and it takes four men to collect all the money!"

—VIA EDWARD MORRIS, WEST ISLIP, NEW YORK

"Apostate!"

© Jonny Hawkins

My father grew up in a small Nebraska town, and one of his favorite stories was about Pastor Nelson. Each Sunday, during the announcements, Pastor Nelson asked everyone to fill out an attendance card and pass it to the side aisle.

The ushers collected the cards during the next hymn, which preceded the sermon. If the pastor forgot an important announcement, someone would write it on the back of a card and pass it to the ushers.

During the sermon, they would take the card to Pastor Nelson, who would read it to the congregation. One day they took him a note written by his wife. Without pause, Pastor Nelson announced to everyone, "Hurry up and get the sermon over with! The roast is burning!"

—BRUCE "CHARLIE" JOHNSON, EDITOR, *THE CLOWN IN TIMES*, KENMORE, WASHINGTON

In the past, *The Joyful Noiseletter* has passed on some fanciful front-page headlines that news media have used after angels of the Lord informed them that the world would end tomorrow. Here are some more headlines via Paul Thigpen of Springfield, Missouri:

Sports Illustrated: "Game's Over"

Ladies' Home Journal: "Lose 10 Pounds by Judgment Day with Our New Armageddon Diet!"

Inc. Magazine: "Ten Ways You Can Profit from the Apocalypse"

Washington Post: "End of World Linked to Republican Contract with America"

Washington Times: "End of World Linked to Whitewater"

CNN: "World Ends; Women and Children Most Affected"

Penney's Catalog: "Our Final Sale"

America Online: "System Temporarily Down, Try Calling Back in 15 Minutes"

◻◻◇

Pastor Mike McClung of Lionheart Fellowship in Maryville, Tennessee, passed along the following "proof that Barney is the Antichrist" in hopes that he might wring a laugh out of prophecy students:

1. Start with the given:
   CUTE PURPLE DINOSAUR
2. Change all the U's to V's (which is proper Latin anyway):
   CVTE PVRPLE DINOSAVR
3. Extract all the Roman Numerals:
   CVVLDIV

4. Convert these to Arabic values:

100-5-5-50-500-1-5

5. Add them up:

666

If man evolved from monkeys and apes, why do we still have monkeys and apes?

—VIA PATTY WOOTEN, RN, SANTA CRUZ, CALIFORNIA

"My wife has been bugging me about church. But, hey, I've got my whole life ahead of me. There's plenty of time for religion."

© Ed Sullivan

The Reverend Steven W. Lawler of St. Louis tells the story of the Chicago Episcopal matron whose daughter returned from her first semester of studying philosophy in college and announced that she was an atheist. The mother replied, "That may all be well and good. But you will be an Episcopal atheist!"

—THE ANGLICAN DIGEST

After his air force and troops demolished Grozny, the capital of rebellious Chechnya, Russian President Boris Yeltsin was being given a tour of the area when he spotted an old Chechen man praying near the rubble of a home.

Yeltsin ordered his chauffeur to stop the limousine.

"You are praying for someone?" Yeltsin asked.

"I am praying for Boris Yeltsin," the old man replied.

"Thank you," Yeltsin said, identifying himself. "You seem old enough to have prayed for Stalin, Lenin, and the Czar. Did you pray for them, too?"

"Yes sir, I did," the old man replied. "And look what happened to them!"

I will have no melancholy or sad spirits in my house. Cheerful people are more easily led to perfection. Persevere in cheerfulness, for this is the true way to make progress in virtue.

—PHILIP NERI (1515-1595)

Classified ad under employment opportunities in a Los Angeles newspaper:

"Position requires: wisdom of Solomon, patience of Job, skill of David. No other applicants have a prayer."

Second Ponce de Leon Baptist Church is located at 2715 Peachtree Street NE in Atlanta, Georgia, between the Catholic Cathedral of Christ the King and the Episcopal Cathedral of St. Philip across the street. Both the Catholics and the Episcopalians held very early services, and parked in the Baptist parking lot so that space was not available for the Baptist Sunday-school arrivals.

A Baptist deacon solved the problem by applying this bumper sticker to all cars that parked there too early before Sunday school: "I'm Proud to Be a Southern Baptist."

Pastor Jeff Byrd, ministry coordinator at the Baptist church, said he has heard the story many times. "It happened long ago," he said. "But there's no problem now. Now we get there earlier than the Catholics and Episcopalians."

—CLARENCE G. DURHAM, MARYVILLE, TENNESSEE

"That sermon today really told the Smiths off!"

"That sermon today really told the Johnsons off!"

© Goddard Sherman

A well-liked minister in a small town church was offered twice his salary to move to a large church in a big city.

A church member encountered the minister's daughter in a

shop. "Is your father going to accept the church's offer in the big city?" the church member asked.

The daughter replied, "I don't know. He's been on his knees praying for divine guidance this morning."

"And what is your mother doing?"

"She's upstairs packing," the daughter said.

—VIA CATHERINE HALL, PITTSBURGH, PENNSYLVANIA

An Israeli tour guide told his group of tourists as they stood among ancient ruins: "This is the site of an ancient synagogue. It was built 2,003 years ago."

The tourists were duly impressed at the precision of the date for the structure. "That's amazing!" said one. "How do you know the exact year?"

"Well," said the guide, "the archaeologist told me it was 2,000 years old, and that was three years ago."

—PAUL THIGPEN, SPRINGFIELD, MISSOURI

A burned-out assistant pastor was advised by his senior pastor to see a Christian counselor. "Do you have trouble making decisions about your sermon themes?" the counselor asked.

"Well...yes and no...," the pastor replied.

—VIA GEORGE GOLDTRAP, ORMOND-BY-THE-SEA, FLORIDA

One priest was so frustrated over the failure of some in the pews to extend their hand at the sign of peace that he threatened to set up "Sign of Peace" and "No Sign of Peace" sections.

—DOLORES CURRAN, ST. ANTHONY MESSENGER

AN ODE TO SICK WORSHIPERS

Barb Hughes lives in Portland, Oregon, with her husband, Chris, and their two children, Aubrey, four, and Toby, two. She wrote the editor of *TJN:* "It seems every time my young family and I go to church, one of us gets sick." So she composed this "Ode to Sick Worshipers."

> She loves little children,
> They're so darlingly cute,
> But she's nursing a cold
> With a throat that's a beaut.
> She gushed as she touched
> Baby's hands and his cheeks.
> Now this haggard young mom
> Has sick babies for weeks.
> He's practiced and honed up
> His part in the choir
> With the low bassy tones
> And the melody higher.
> His singing is splendid,
> His harmony true,
> But the choir won't appreciate
> Sharing his flu.
> Even "Miss Careful" who
> Washes and lathers
> Can't get away from
> The sickness-germ-passers.
> She's discovered the
> Cleanest protection is fleeting

When shaking ill hands
During meeting and greeting.
You are a timely and
Needed church member,
In church every month —
As long as remembered.
But if your eyes or nose
Or your throat is so red,
You should be home,
With your tissues, in bed.
This sincere thought's
From a Mom and a Dad
And meant to protect us,
Our dear lass, and our lad.
We hope that you listen
to this little poem —
If you are sick, please
Be kind and **stay home!**

—BARB HUGHES

A woman from Maine was visiting her family at Christmastime in a small town in the South. She was surprised to find in the town square a crèche with the Three Wise Men wearing firefighters' helmets.

At a nearby church, she stopped and asked the secretary why the Three Wise Men were wearing helmets. She said she couldn't recall reading anything about firefighters in the Bible when Jesus was born.

"You Yankees never read the Bible!" the woman said, angrily.

She took out a Bible, flipped through some pages, and pointed at a passage. "Look!" she said. "It says right here, 'The Three Wise Men came from afar.'"

A DAILY PRAYER: I want to thank you, Lord, for being close to me so far this day. With your help I haven't been impatient, lost my temper, been grumpy, judgmental, or envious of anyone. But I will be getting out of bed in a minute, and I think I will really need your help then. Amen.

—DEAN ALAN JONES
CHURCH OF THE RISEN CHRIST BULLETIN,
DENVER, COLORADO

© Dennis Daniel

2

Out of the Mouths of God's Kids

"You're the theology expert around here... can we baptize Beanie Babies?"

© Jonny Hawkins

A small child with a bad cough was taken by her parents to a hospital emergency room.

A nurse, examining the child's lungs with a stethoscope, told the child: "I have to see if Barney is in there."

"I have Jesus in my heart," the child replied. "Barney is on my underwear."

—VIA PATTY WOOTEN, RN, SANTA CRUZ, CALIFORNIA

Three-year-old Nick was especially fond of his great-grandfather. When he died, Nick's mother explained to him that the grandfather had gone to Heaven.

"Mom, Grandpa is with God, right?" Nick said.

"Yes, his mother replied.

"Well, why doesn't God fix him and send him back?"

—*Springfield (Missouri) News-Leader,*
via Paul Thigpen

After a four-year-old boy told his father that he had a stomachache, the father suggested: "That's because it's empty. You'd feel better if you had something in it." He gave the child a glass of juice.

A couple of days later, the family's pastor came by to visit the family. The pastor mentioned that he had a bad headache.

The little boy responded: "That's because it's empty. You'd feel better if you had something in it."

—via Rev. Warren Keating, First Presbyterian
Church, Derby, Kansas

Hank Billings, columnist for the *Springfield (Missouri) News-Leader,* says a fellow church member told him the first time his granddaughter saw the Oral Roberts University campus in Tulsa, she was very impressed by the futuristic prayer tower. "Look," she exclaimed, "it's the home of the Jetsons!"

—via Paul Thigpen, Springfield, Missouri

One of the mothers at St. John's Evangelical Lutheran Church in Lewistown, Pennsylvania, happened to drive by the home of

Pastor Gerald A. Krum while he was mowing his lawn. Her six-year-old daughter stared out the car window in open-mouthed amazement.

"Isn't that Pastor Krum mowing the grass?" she asked.

"Yes, her mother said. "What's wrong with that?"

"I thought he could just ask God not to make it grow," the little girl answered.

A Sunday school teacher asked the children just before she dismissed them to go to church, "And why is it necessary to be quiet in church?"

Annie replied, "Because people are sleeping."

—MARTHA J. BECKMAN

The Sunday school teacher at our church, Sunrise Church in Rialto, California, was telling the little children in her class that God loves them all the time, even when they're grumpy.

"And Happy!" exclaimed Jeremy, my two-year-old-grandson, adding, "...and Sleepy and Dopey and Sneezy and Doc and Bashful."

—CAROL A. REASONER

> The Angel that presided o'er my birth
> Said, "Little creature, formed of joy and mirth,
> Go love without the help of any thing on earth."
> —WILLIAM BLAKE

When a pastor heard a little boy use a cuss word, he said, "Son, every time I hear you swear, a cold chill runs down my back."

"Gee," said the boy, "if you had been at our house yesterday when Dad caught his finger in the door, you'd have frozen to death!"

—JIM REED, COTTER, ARKANSAS

After the christening of his baby brother in church, a three-year-old boy sobbed all the way home in the backseat of the car. His father asked him three times what was wrong.

Finally, the boy replied: "That preacher said he wanted us brought up in a Christian home, and I wanted to stay with you guys."

—THE CHARLOTTE OBSERVER, VIA ANITA CHICHESTER, CONCORD, NORTH CAROLINA

"Before I tell you what happened, Mom, remember... The Lord will never give you more than you can handle."

© Bill Frauhiger

When I was a young pastor at Mount Pleasant Baptist Church between Richmond and Williamsburg, Virginia, I spoke earnestly one Sunday on the need for Christians to get back to the basics of their faith. Later, a church member's child was asked at Sunday dinner what the pastor's sermon was about. The little girl replied, "He talked about going back and getting the biscuits."

—CHAPLAIN SHIELDS MOORE, INTERFAITH CHAPEL, TAMPA (FLORIDA) INTERNATIONAL AIRPORT

Rev. Dr. Geoff Pankhurst of Orange, Australia, says his wife, a teacher, was telling her primary school class about Saint Francis and how he had taken a vow of poverty. "Who can tell me what a vow is?" she asked.

A small girl raised her hand and replied: "A and e and..."

One Sunday morning, I was sitting in church right behind the pastor's spouse and their two children. When the pastor entered the pulpit, the seven-year-old son asked his mother if he could be excused so that he could go to the nursery.

His mother replied: "No, you're too old to go to the nursery."

The pastor's son protested loudly, "But Mom, I heard it last night and it's a long one."

—REV. VIRGINIA K. BARNES, ST. MATTHEW'S LUTHERAN CHURCH, JACKSONVILLE, FLORIDA

Rev. Warren J. Keating of the First Presbyterian Church in Derby, Kansas, told this story, which happened in the office of a family physician where Reverend Keating's wife works as a nurse:

A farm family—the mother, her six-year-old son, and three-year-old daughter—came to see the doctor because all three of them had been ill with the flu. The grandmother accompanied them.

The doctor explained that the mother and children needed to rest because they were sick.

"My grandma is sick too," the little boy said.

"No, your grandma is not sick," the doctor said.

"Oh yes she is," the boy said. "She's depressed."

The mother added: "Yes, the children have been praying for Grandma and her depression."

The little boy turned to his grandma and said, "I'm sorry to tell you this, Grandma, but you're going to be depressed for six more months."

"Why do you say that, honey?" his grandma asked.

"Well," the boy said, "I've been praying for a calf for six months and I just now got it!"

FIRSTBORN

I hold this flannel-wrapped miracle

Close to my heart

Lullabying love, as I begin

The mile in my mother's moccasins.

—DONA MADDUX COOPER, *FAMILY TIES,*
STILLWATER, OKLAHOMA

When their daughter Debby was two years old, Joanne Hinch of Woodland Hills, California, and her husband, a Presbyterian minister, invited a Catholic priest to Sunday dinner.

While Debby helped her mother bake a cake for the dinner, they practiced saying their guest's name, Monsignor Keating. After much practice on Debby's part, it continued to come out "Monster Keating."

"Let's just call him Father Keating," her mother finally said.

That seemed fine with Debby, but that evening, shortly before dinner, she asked, "Well, isn't Mother Keating coming?"

◊

Joshua is a talkative four-year-old boy in our church, Covenant Moravian Church in York, Pennsylvania. I have a weekly "children's chat" during our worship services. On the Sunday when we celebrated the baptism of Jesus, I went to the baptismal font and asked the children, "What do we do here?"

Joshua yelled out, "Baptize! That's where you sprinkled water on my head, Pastor Dean!"

I told the children that next Sunday we were going to baptize little Joey there. The next week, Joshua greeted me before Sunday school and announced, "Pastor Dean, today is the day Joey gets paradised!"

Later, after Joey had been baptized, Joshua came up for the children's chat, and asked: "Did you finish pulverizing Joey?"

—REV. DEAN JURGEN

Ruth Anderson, council president of Covenant Community Church in Akron, Ohio, took her four-year-old granddaughter from Massachusetts into her Ohio home while her parents were on vacation. Although her parents are not regular churchgoers, her grandparents are, and they took the girl to Sunday school and church on two Sundays.

When her parents returned, the girl was eager to tell them all that she had done. "They have a place that they go to here in Ohio," she told them. "They call it church."

—KARL HARSNEY, CUYAHOGA FALLS, OHIO

"Now that God has told you to spare my life, Dad, can I have an allowance increase?"

© Andrew Toos

Margie Squires, a Sunday school teacher at Hunter Community Church, Franklin, Ohio, was teaching her preschool class the story of Moses. Tyler, one of the youngsters, was constantly introducing the movie monster Godzilla into every lesson. That morning, Tyler insisted that Godzilla was going to save her from Moses' burning bush. Finally, another little girl asked, "Is Zilla God's last name?"

—REV. VERNON BABCOCK

FMC member Rev. John Savukynas of St. Mary's Church, Plano, Illinois, visited the children in the church school kindergarten one day and thought he would have a little fun with them.

He told the children: "King Herod wanted to kill Baby Jesus. An angel appeared to Joseph in a dream and said, 'Get up and take the child and his mother and flee to Egypt.' Joseph got up and took the child and his mother and left that night for Egypt. What happened to the flea?"

A little girl raised her hand and answered: "It went to the flea market."

In church with his mother, a small child was fascinated by the stained-glass windows. "Who are those people painted on the windows," the boy asked.

"Those are saints," his mother replied. When he went home, he told his father that he had seen the saints in church.

"Who are the saints?" his dad asked.

"Saints are people the light shines through," the boy said.

—VIA REV. PAUL R. GRAVES,
SANDPOINT, IDAHO

During a discussion of Creation, Darleen Anderson of Springfield, Missouri, asked her four-year-old grandson, Shane: "Which came first, the chicken or the egg?"

"Oh, Grandma, God was really first," Shane replied, and then added, "but were you second?"

—SPRINGFIELD (MISSOURI) NEWS-LEADER,
VIA PAUL THIGPEN

Poor Adam and Eve

Had another claim to fame:

They were the first, ever,

To raise a little Cain.

—JEANE C. GOTTSPONER, YUMA, ARIZONA

How many youth pastors does it take to change a light bulb?
Answer: None. They don't stay long enough to change a light bulb.

© Steve Phelps

When I began my sermon one Sunday, it became obvious that my young son was fidgety. His mother whispered to him, "Please be quiet. You are not supposed to talk during church."

He immediately stood in the pew, pointed directly at me, and declared in a loud voice, "Well, Daddy is talking!"

—REV. ROBERT R. ALLEN, CAMP HOPEWELL,
OXFORD, MISSISSIPPI

Vonnie O'Connor of Lawton, Michigan, took her two young sons on a field trip to see the relics of some saints at Nazareth convent's Holy Family Chapel. The nuns of the Sisters of St. Joseph had collected the relics—pieces of bones, mostly—over the years.

Joe, age nine, asked his mother how the nuns knew these were actually the bones of the saints.

David, age seven, answered, "Because the sisters were alive at that time!"

JUST A PIDDLIN' POEM

Once there was a little lad,
Always in a rush.
In fact, in such a hurry
That he'd forget to flush.
His mother would remind him,
And sometimes she would scold.
And even when she threatened,
He'd forget what he'd been told.
One day exasperated,
She called up to the school,
Told his teacher to send him home
So he could flush the stool.
On the playground was the culprit,
So Miss Marks yelled loud and clear
From the second-story window,
Those words for all to hear.
Never was a face more reddened.

Never ran two feet so fast.

Surely, this third-grader

Had, a lesson, learned at last.

But many decades later,

His lawful wedded wife

Has been known to say that he still leads

A fast and flushless life.

—DONA MADDUX COOPER, *FAMILY TIES*,
STILLWATER, OKLAHOMA

Pastor Wallace seriously entertains the thought of hiring a youth director.

The youth minister was using the visual aid of a flashlight to make his point during the children's sermon. "We are to be the light of the world even as Jesus was," he told the children.

He had filled the inside of the flashlight with junk, which he proceeded to empty. Inserting batteries which he had labeled "Jesus," he observed: "When we have Jesus in our hearts, we become lights." He turned on the flashlight, but nothing happened.

A little boy exclaimed in a loud voice: "It won't work unless you screw the head on straight."

—REV. JAMES M. LOGAN, FEDERATED CHURCH OF
GREEN LAKE, MICHIGAN

> A cheerful heart is a good medicine,
>
> but a downcast spirit dries up the bones.
>
> —PROVERBS 17:22, RSV

"It's 10 o'clock. Do you know where your child-like faith is?"

© Jonny Hawkins

FMC member Clint Kelly's book *How to Win Grins and Influence Little People* (Honor Books) has this advice for nurturing our little ones:

- Grab your child in a bear-hug and say, "You are a living miracle!"
- Ask your child to laugh for you, then say, "I love that sound. It makes me want to laugh too."
- Leave a note on the bathroom mirror. "Good morning, Brenda, what a fine smile you have!"
- Record your child's laughter, and play it back once in a while. Say, "Now that's music to my ears!"
- Say, "You're so much fun to be with. Let's play!"

3

Bloopers That Gnash the Teeth

"Did you know that your pianist just played a Billy Joel tune as the offertory?"

© Dik LaPine

For centuries, theologians have blamed demons for misprints and typographical errors, while pastors and church secretaries have been inclined to blame one another. Even with the most meticulous readings and proofreadings by several persons, misprints abound in church bulletins, newsletters, and publications. Here are some more of our favorite bloopers:

In the bulletin of Saint Elizabeth Ann Seton Catholic Church, Palm Coast, Florida:

"We will have a Special Holiday Bingo & Dinner on Monday evening, December 30. You will be given 2 Bingo packs which cover all games played, and your choice of children or roast beef for dinner."

—VIA REV. FREDERICK R. PARKE

From a church bulletin:

"Eight new choir robes are needed due to the addition of several new members and the deterioration of some older ones."

—VIA GEORGE GOLDTRAP, ORMOND-BY-THE-SEA, FLORIDA

From a church bulletin:

"Low Self-Esteem Support Group will meet at 8 P.M. Wednesday. Please use the back door."

—VIA PATTY WOOTEN, RN, SANTA CRUZ, CALIFORNIA

From the Dalton (Georgia) Daily Citizen News:

"John _____, ordained as a deamon, will pastor two churches in Fannin County."

—VIA REV. DUSTIN PENNINGTON, FIRST ASSEMBLY OF GOD, DALTON, GEORGIA

Classified ad in the Criterion, *Catholic archdiocesan newspaper of Indianapolis:*

"Christian live-in female companion needed by older lady. Must have ear."

—VIA JOSEPH L. HENLEY, BEDFORD, INDIANA

Blooper in a Catholic church bulletin:

"Father _____has spoken in the largest Catholic churches in America. To miss hearing him will be the chance of a lifetime."

—VIA JOSEPH A. MAHER, OXNARD, CALIFORNIA

Blooper in April 12, 1998 Sunday bulletin of Crystal Cathedral, Garden Grove, California:

"Remember in Prayer:
Matilda _____, awaiting surgery to remove large brain behind the eye."

—VIA DR. JACK W. TALLMAN, TUSTIN, CALIFORNIA

People with a sense of humor tend to be less egocentric. They are more humble in moments of success and less defeated in times of travail.

—COMEDIAN BOB NEWHART

Dr. Alan C. Rhodes of Grace United Methodist Church, Ravena, New York, spotted this blooper in his hometown newspaper, the Press-Republican *of Plattsburgh, New York:*

"_____is consecrated today as the eighth bishop of the Episcopal Diocese of Albany at the New York State Convention Center. The Presiding Bishop of the Episcopal Church of the United States leads other bishops, parish priests, deacons, and laity in the festive occasion. It continues the church's tradition of an unbroken line of apostasy dating back to the original twelve apostles."

◌◌
◌

During the dark days of World War II, a devout Frenchman in the underground telegraphed this message to supporters in England:

"God reigns!" But the message was garbled in transit and came out "God resigns!" The English wired back: "Regret decision. British policy remains the same."

—VIA *THE ANGLICAN DIGEST*

"Eternal damnation? Do you realize how this will look on my resumé?"

© Harley L. Schwadron

In the bulletin of Peace Lutheran Church, Smyrna, Delaware:

"Pray for our church and Pastor and Mrs. Krompart as we consider their proposal to help us here at Peace. Let's not sit back and take them for granite, but, receive, welcome and work with them."

—VIA REV. JAMES A. LANGE, LEWES, DELAWARE

From a minister's letter published in a farm magazine:

"I have pestered rural churches for nearly thirty years."

—VIA REV. DENNY BRAKE, RALEIGH, NORTH CAROLINA

The closing worship chorus at Ames United Methodist Church in Saginaw, Michigan, was the majestic "The Dwelling of God Is Among You Today." But the worshipers doubled over with laughter when they read the lines in the church bulletin:

"And then I heard a loud voice say,
'Behold, the dwelling of God is among you today!
'And He shall wipe away your rears....'"

—LAWRENCE C. BROOKS, SAGINAW, MICHIGAN

The annual report of the female president to the congregation of First English Lutheran Church, Kimball, Nebraska, declared:

"We as a congregation have achieved many accomplishments. We have been truly blessed in our missions and ministry. All of the broads have done an excellent job."

—MRS. DWAYNE HUNZEKER, KIMBALL, NEBRASKA

Rev. Henry E. Riley Jr., of Chesterfield, Virginia passed on this story from the last century when typesetters used movable hottype. The typesetter of an English newspaper mixed up the lead slugs on two news stories — one reporting on a new pig-killing-sausage-making machine and the other reporting on a pastor's retirement party. Here's how the story appeared in the newspaper:

"Several of the Reverend Dr. Mudge's friends called upon him yesterday, and after a conversation, the unsuspecting pig was seized by the hind leg and slid along a beam until he reached the hot water tank.... Thereupon he came forward and said that there were times when the feelings overpowered one, and for that reason, he would not attempt to do more than thank those around him for the manner in which such a huge animal was cut into fragments was simply astonishing.

"The doctor concluded his remarks, when the machine seized him and in less time than it takes to write it, the pig was cut into fragments and worked up into delicious sausage. The occasion will be long remembered by the doctor's friends as one of the most delightful of their lives. The best pieces can be procured for tenpence a pound, and we are sure that those who have sat so long under his ministry will rejoice that he has been treated so handsomely."

◇

A computerized letter promoting *Country Woman* magazine was sent to the First Baptist Church of Chapman, Nebraska, addressed to "Mrs. First B Church," with the salutation: "Dear Mrs. First Church."

—LLOYD BOYCE, PASTOR

The Very Reverend Robert A. L'Homme, Dean of Saint Paul's Episcopal Cathedral, Diocese of Quincy, Peoria, Illinois, reports he once received a computerized letter addressed to "The Very Reverend Fat L'Homme," with the salutation "Dear Fat Father L'Homme."

"At the time, he recalls, "I was 5' 8" tall and weighed 125 pounds. I still ate light that day."

The church bulletin of Westminster Presbyterian Church in Portland, Oregon, carried the following note from Mrs. Roma Church, 80, who had been hospitalized: "Thank you so very much, my dead friends, for the lovely cards, phone calls, and visits during my recent accident and subsequent recovery. Hope to be with you soon. Lovingly, Roma."

—VIA BUD FRIMOTH, PORTLAND, OREGON

"I don't know what the preacher's got against procrastination... I thought that was one of our main doctrines."

© Dennis Daniel

In the January 27 bulletin of Hillcrest (Illinois) Christian Church, Pastor Julie Durkin-Pigg wrote: "The snowfall of 6-7 inches kept us homebound a few days; serious illnesses have kept many occupied; the pastor lost her vice for over a week and then spent another two weeks coughing non-stop."

—VIA DICK FRIEDLINE, ORANGE, CALIFORNIA

In the bulletin of the Comstock, Michigan, Church of Christ:

"'Come, Christian, Join to Sin' Vs. All No. 55."

—VIA JOANNA BARNES, KALAMAZOO, MICHIGAN

Blooper in a Catholic church bulletin:

"The church had a going-away party for Father _____. The congregation was anxious to give him a little momentum."

—VIA JOSEPH A. MAHER, OXNARD, CALIFORNIA

Reverend Sheldon patiently waits for an apology from the chairman of the board.

© Steve Phelps

> If you're going to be able to look back on something and laugh about it, you might as well laugh about it now.
>
> —MARIE OSMOND

Classified ad in the Nickel Ads *in Wenatchee, Washington:*

"Newer Wood church pews, sleeps six, $100 each. (509) 884-3293."

—VIA LES FOLTZ JR., BELLEVUE, WASHINGTON

The other day I saw a T-shirt that had a map of York County, Pennsylvania, on it with little crosses all over it. Beneath the map was this message: "York County, Pennsylvania...where Lutherans are the densest." (According to ELCA statistics, York County does have the highest concentration of Lutherans per unit area.)

—RONALD LEESE, SPRING GROVE, PENNSYLVANIA

"I forget – did you want *three* copies of the three sins caused by original sin, or *one* copy of the original sermon on the three *causes* of original sin?"

© Ed Sullivan

From *Good News Letter* of Hoyle Memorial United Methodist Church, Shelby, North Carolina, this headline referring to a problem with the parsonage heating system:

"Parsonage Hearing System Replaced."

—REV. RICHARD C. CLOUGH JR., PASTOR

Carole A. Loll, a Stephen minister at First Presbyterian Church in Jackson, Michigan, discovered this blooper in the 1997 annual report of the church's property committee:

"Something was finally done about the sidewalk along the east side of the building. We had a handrail installed to assist people negotiating this hell. Hopefully, we will see fewer slips and falls this winter."

Fr. Gabriel Calvo, founder of the Marriage Encounter movement, was quoted in Marriage *magazine as follows:*

"Our reward is to realize that with the generous and loving cooperation of so many team couples, priests, rabies, and bene-factors that millions of married couples all over the world have been able to experience a Marriage Encounter weekend."

The unison prayer in a church appeared as follows:

"We find our world a clod and cheerless place without your love."

—DR. JOHN F. CLIFFORD, FIRST UNITED METHODIST CHURCH, COMANCHE, TEXAS

FMC member Rev. Robert M. Thompson, senior pastor at Corinth Reformed United Church of Christ in Hickory, North Carolina, researched some old church minutes from several years ago when there was a period of conflict in the church over sending money to the denomination. The secretary taking the minutes quoted one member as saying, "There should be a goodwill or faith statement made by Corinth in the fact that we will financially support our domination."

In the "Fifth Sunday after Pentecost" church bulletin of Congregational United Church of Christ, Lewiston, Michigan: "O loving God, who reaches out to restore our soles, touch us now with your word of truth…"

In the bulletin of the Raymore (Missouri) Christian Church (Disciples of Christ), an article appeared that began:

"Visioning Conferences. Under the leadership of Dr. Paul Diehl, we will follow the book *Twelve Keys to an Effective Church*…"

Directly below the article, another item appeared with the headline: "Please Return Church Keys." The item requested: "If you possess a church key which you no longer use as a Moderator, please return it to the church office."

—VIA REV. LARRY LEA ODOM-GROH, FIRST
CHRISTIAN CHURCH, CHILLICOTHE, MISSOURI

From the January bulletin of Ascension Lutheran Church, Thousand Oaks, California:

"My 1998 Resolution Calendar. With the help of God I resolve to: Be a good wittiness to those around me by what I say and through what I do..."

—VIA TED L. HULBERT, ROCKAWAY, OREGON

> Those who are wise overlook many wrongs and often do not take them as such, for either they do not know about them or, if they do, they make fun of them and turn them into jokes. To pay no attention to injuries is a mark of magnanimity.
>
> —MARTIN OF BRAGA

© Steve Phelps

4

St. Murphy's Commandments

A seminarian looks ahead | A pastor looks back

The Joyful Noiseletter *consulting editor Ron Birk—a San Marcos, Texas, goat rancher, Lutheran pastor, humorist, and speaker—is the author of a book called* St. Murphy's Commandments, *a collection of observations about church life. Following are some samples of* St. Murphy's Commandments, © *1997 by Ron Birk. LangMarc Publishing, San Antonio, Texas. Reprinted with permission.*

After my own extensive research into the subject, I hereby submit "St. Murphy's Commandments"—laws in the church that are akin to Murphy's Law: "If anything can go wrong, it will."

"St. Murphy's Commandments" pertain to pastors and the relationship they have with their congregations.

- *The Hunger-for-Quiet Precept:* Stomachs growl only during silent prayers.
- *The First Myth of Organized Religion:* Religion is not organized.
- *The Cool-It Concept:* In an air-conditioned church, the number of men who are too warm will be equal to the number of women who are too cool.
- *The Airer-of-Your-Ways Warning:* Never make confession to a pastor wearing a microphone.
- *St. Murphy's Commandment:* Anything a preacher says that can be misunderstood will be misunderstood.
- *The Seminary Curriculum Commandment:* The one thing they didn't teach in seminary is the first thing a pastor will need to know on the job.
- *The Rule of Emerging Emergencies:* Emergencies arise in direct proportion to the fullness of the pastor's schedule.
- *The Rule of Researching Religiously:* Read enough theological books and you will find someone who supports your beliefs. *Corollary:* Have enough Bible translations in your library and you will find one that agrees with what you think a particular passage says.
- *The Don't-Push Postulate:* The more obvious it is what a pastor wants a congregation to do, the less likely they are to do it.
- *The Judgment Judgment:* A pastor's good judgment grows in direct proportion to the number of bad judgments made.
- *The Axiom of Availability:* Church members really don't care what pastors do with their time, except that pastors

be readily available whenever the member needs them.

- *The Dogma Dictum:* Let sleeping dogmas lie.
- *The You-Can't-Win-for-Losing Law:* Pastors never win church arguments.
- *The Law of Longevity:* Pastors leave, congregations stay.
- *The Dictum of Don't-Do-Too-Much:* Pastors should never do what a layperson can do.
- *The That's-The-Way-You-Learn Law:* Every experienced pastor began with no experience.
- *The First Law of Liturgical Leadership:* If you can't chant, don't!
- *The Clothes-Don't-Make-the-Pastor Rule:* A colorful clerical doesn't always make a cleric colorful.
- *The Those-Who-Have-Ears-to-Hear-Have-Heard Law:* Experienced pastors are never surprised at what they hear in a counseling session.
- *The Never-Too-Late Law:* For pastors there is no such thing as the last phone call of the day.
- *The Watch-What-You-Say Commandment:* No one will remember everything a pastor says, but everything a pastor says will be remembered by someone. *Corollary:* There will always be someone who remembers the pastor saying something the pastor doesn't remember saying.
- *The More-Help-the-More-Work Principle:* The more people there are to help pastors do their jobs, the more a pastor's job becomes helping those helping pastors do their jobs.
- *The Law of Speaking Out:* The surest way for a pastor to find out how many members are against an issue is to speak out for that issue.
- *The Dangers-of-Change Theorem:* The more a pastor works

for change in a congregation, the more likely the congregation will change pastors.

- *The Unexpected-Solo Rule:* There is an inverse relationship between the pastor's favorite hymn and the congregation's ability to sing that hymn.
- *The You-Can't-Please 'em-All Axiom:* When pastors try to please everyone, they don't. *Corollary:* No two members have the same expectations of the pastor.
- *The Too-Close-for-Comfort Commandment:* No parsonage can be too far from the church.
- *The I-Can-Do-Something-Right Rule:* Incompetent senior pastors often hire able assistant pastors.
- *The Bishop-on-a-Hot-Tin-Roof Rule:* Nothing is worse than a nervous bishop, especially when you are the one who is making the bishop nervous.

"They're either having a board meeting or a Stooge Fest."

5

Signs and Wonders

© Jonny Hawkins

Seen on an outdoor church sign:

"The Lord is seeking righteous fruit, not religious nuts."

—VIA REV. LARRY CRAWFORD, WESTLAKE CHRISTIAN
FELLOWSHIP, ST. CHARLES, MARYLAND

Sign seen outside the Lighthouse Baptist Church in St. Louis:

"If you're looking for a sign from God, this is it."

—VIA RICHARD J. SCHULER, SAINT PETERS, MISSOURI

Bumper sticker seen by Edward W. Avery Jr., Rye, New York:

"As Long As There Are Tests, There Will Be Prayer in Public Schools."

Sign seen outside Needier Church of Christ in Haleyville, Alabama:

"God so loved the world that He did not send a committee."

On a bumper sticker in Indianapolis:

"Jesus Is Coming! Look Busy!"

A gospel group called The Resurrection was scheduled to sing at the Barlow (Kentucky) First Baptist Church, but the performance was postponed because of a snowstorm. The pastor put up an outside sign that read: "The Resurrection is postponed."

—VIA MARIA VILLALOVOS, PICO RIVERA, CALIFORNIA

On Thanksgiving Day, FMC member Bill Reynolds of Palatka, Florida, saw this church sign as he drove by the First Baptist Church in San Mateo, Florida.

"11-26-97 Services Canceled
In Everything Give Thanks"

Bumper sticker spotted by George Goldtrap of Ormond-by-the-Sea, Florida:

"The More You Complain, the Longer God Lets You Live."

Sign outside a San Diego church:

"Will it take six strong pallbearers to bring you back?"

Outdoor sign at a church in Lachine, Quebec, announcing Sunday's sermon:

"Escape from God
Come Worship With Us"

—CANADIAN BAPTIST

> Life is a mirror: if you frown at it, it frowns back; if you smile, it returns the greeting.
>
> —WILLIAM THACKERAY

Oh stop your whining and grow up!

A sure sign your pastor
is ready for a vacation

© Steve Phelps

A pastor hired a painter to paint a sign for the church. The painter painted a sign which read: "Church of Christ."

The pastor saw the sign and was very unhappy. "This is not a Church of Christ," he scolded the painter.

So the sign painter reworded the sign to say: "This is not a Church of Christ."

This time the pastor was furious. Exasperated, the painter packed his tools and told the pastor: "When you make up your mind, call me!"

—GEORGE GOLDTRAP

Rev. Paul R. Graves of Sandpoint, Idaho, recently walked into the men's rest room in Sandpoint United Methodist Church and saw this professionally lettered sign on the wall next to the toilet: "Guest Parking."

◇

On the way to work, J. Douglas Parks of Lexington, Kentucky, saw the following sign directing people to St. Andrew's United Methodist Church in Nicholasville, Kentucky:

"Turn to the Lord
Left at the traffic light."

◇

Lowell J. Goering reports the following sign is posted on the entry doors to his church, Trinity Mennonite Church, of Hillsboro, Kansas:

"Leave your frown out here.
Leave your cares in there.
Bring your smile out here.
And spread it everywhere."

© Harley L. Schwadron

Seen on an outdoor church sign:

"You aren't too bad to come in;
You aren't good enough to stay out."

—VIA MYLES AND PHYLLIS WEBER,
FOX POINT, WISCONSIN

Sign seen in front of a church:

"God bless America—and please hurry!"

—VIA CATHERINE HALL,
PITTSBURGH, PENNSYLVANIA

On a sign in front of Emanuel Baptist Church in Waco, Texas:

"Welcome to Eternity—Smoking or Non-Smoking?"

—GEORGE GOLDTRAP

Two adjacent signs seen at the top of a large bookshelf in a Christian bookstore in Decatur, Illinois:

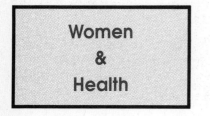

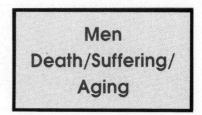

Hazel Bimler of Itasca, Illinois, spotted this sign at Christmastime at Women's Work Out World:

"Merry Fitness—Happy New Rear!"

Seen on a church's outdoor sign:

"Board broken. Message inside."

—VIA REV. KARL KRAFT, MANTUA, NEW JERSEY

Bumper sticker suggested by Mary Rucinski, Westford, Massachusetts:

"God Loves You Anyway"

"Yes, his work is known throughout many church circles. It is riveting, rare and insightful. He wrote the best bumper sticker I've ever read."

© Jonny Hawkins

Humor is surely an essential ingredient in my work and well-being as a mental health chaplain and child of God. Perhaps we should make a new bumper sticker that says: "Humor Happens"

—REV. ROGER P. FROBE, CHAPLAIN
MOCCASIN BEND MENTAL HEALTH INSTITUTE,
CHATTANOOGA, TENNESSEE

FMC member Jeanette Silva of Scott Bar, California, says she wears a button that declares:

"WARNING: Humor may be hazardous to your illness."

Heavy thoughts bring on physical maladies.

—MARTIN LUTHER VIA REV. NORMAN E. PORATH,
SCHUYLER, NEBRASKA

6

You Might Be a Preacher If...

"I'd like permission to play God with my staff for just a short time tomorrow."

© Steve Phelps

The best-selling book You Might Be a Preacher If..., volume 2, *by Stan Toler, senior pastor of Trinity Church of the Nazarene, Oklahoma City, and Mark Toler-Hollingsworth offers the following guidelines (reprinted with permission of the authors and Albury Publishing, Tulsa, Oklahoma © 1997):*

You might be a preacher if...

• You've ever seen an "In Memory of..." plate over a commode.

- Everybody has all the answers, but you get stuck with all the questions.
- Everybody stops talking when you enter the room.
- You've ever lied at a funeral.
- You hate beepers and cellular phones.
- You thank the Lord every day for Caller ID.
- You always read the obituaries.
- You've ever suffered an anxiety attack while playing Bible Trivial Pursuit.
- You wonder why people who have some time to kill want to spend it with you.
- You get your second wind when you say, "And in conclusion..."
- You read Lamentations on Monday mornings for devotions.
- The church of your dreams has turned into a nightmare.
- The ideas you bounce off of board members really do.
- Your car tires are balding faster than your head.
- You wish someone would steal some of your sheep.
- You've seen more religion at a pool hall than you've seen at a church softball game.
- Your Bible has more side notes than printed text.
- "Annual church meeting" and "Armageddon" are one and the same to you.
- You've taught people everything you know, and they still act stupid.
- You would live your life over again and do the same things and work 1,000 hours a week—all for half the pay and recognition you get now.

Joy is prayer. Joy is strength. Joy is love. The best way to show my gratitude to God is to accept everything, even my problems, with joy. Never let anything so fill you with sorrow as to make you forget for one moment the joy of Christ risen.

—MOTHER TERESA

"You've been selected as pastor of the month."

© Ed Sullivan

When you affirm big, believe big, and pray big, big things happen.

—NORMAN VINCENT PEALE

7

How Not to Move a Defiant Waterbed

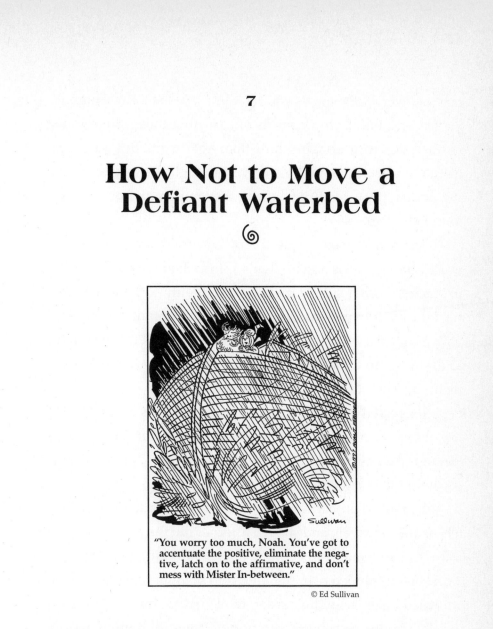

"You worry too much, Noah. You've got to accentuate the positive, eliminate the negative, latch on to the affirmative, and don't mess with Mister In-between."

© Ed Sullivan

The Joyful Noiseletter *consulting editor Liz Curtis Higgs is the Protestant Erma Bombeck. The following two stories were excerpted from her hilarious book* Help! I'm Laughing and I Can't Get Up. *(Reprinted with permission of Thomas Nelson Publishers, Nashville, Tennessee. © 1998 Liz Curtis Higgs)*

Genuinely funny stories usually have their roots in the truth, because everybody knows you can't beat real life for real humor.

Iris and Bill, from Pennsylvania, were moving their young son's possessions from his third-floor apartment. Bill was a professional truck driver, who'd driven all night—twelve exhausting hours. It was late August, and the temperature outside had hit ninety degrees.

Their son owned a queen-size waterbed that took up so much space that Iris and Bill had to slosh their way across it just to reach the other side of the room. Suddenly, the pine box that held the bladder collapsed onto the floor, dropping six hundred gallons of encased water onto their feet. They knew they'd have to drain it before they could ever hope to get it out of the apartment, but they didn't have a siphon handy.

Bill decided they could push this humongous water balloon out the bedroom door, turn a 90-degree corner, and force it through the bathroom door to the shower, where he could simply hold the spout open and it would drain.

Bill grabbed onto the end of the waterbed bladder, braced his feet against the wall, and shoved a corner out the door. It slipped from his hand and slopped back, almost knocking him over.

Then he crawled over that full, cold bladder to the other side and tried again, shoving harder, while Iris sat on the floor near the door trying to compress it, hoping to make it more narrow so it would fit through the door.

Iris glanced up to see hubby's face, the color of a ripe tomato, and she started to laugh when all at once the whole bladder sloshed back—whump!—pinning her underneath it.

Can't you see the headline now? "Woman Killed by Full Bladder."

Her husband lifted the edge enough for her to crawl out. Then they shoved and pulled for another ninety minutes, finally forcing the bladder out the bedroom door toward the kitchen. The bladder took advantage of its sudden freedom and took off—slop, gurgle, slurp, plop—not stopping until it reached the far side of the kitchen, traveling ten feet all by itself.

By now Iris was laughing hysterically and Bill was getting angrier as he feverishly pushed and shoved the six-hundred-gallon body of water. Another hour passed before they forced it across the kitchen and they reached the bathroom doorway.

They pushed, shoved, pulled, and jumped to get it to move through that tiny bathroom door. No luck. Bill leaped like a frog from the kitchen onto the bladder, bounced off, rolled into the bathroom, and hit the wall.

All of a sudden the bladder moved. Half of it went through the bathroom door so fast and so hard that it hit the pipes under a little freestanding sink. Slopping back, it pinned Bill to the shower stall.

Bill whipped out his hunting knife, grabbed that waterbed like it was a wild boar, and cut the end off in one fell swoop, prepared for an explosion of water. The water barely moved. It was at best a trickle. Out came the knife again. A bigger hole. Even so, it took four hours to drain the bladder, which added up to one very long day.

Iris couldn't stop laughing, and every time she looked at her husband, she'd start anew. The bladder, meanwhile, died a slow, painful death, drop by drop, oblivious—or is that *o-blob-ious?*—of the havoc it had created.

THE CASE OF THE MISSING ICE-CREAM CONE

Judy from California shares a story about a woman who was standing in line at an ice-cream store in coastal California when Robert Redford strolled in. (Sigh.) He walked up behind her in line, and the woman decided to play it cool.

She turned, smiled, said hello, then turned back and placed her order. After she paid for her cone and went outside, she realized she didn't have her ice cream.

Robert Redford was still waiting in line when the woman went back in, got the counter girl's attention, and told her she hadn't given her the cone.

The girl answered, "Yes I did, ma'am. You put it in your purse."

Could this have happened? You bet. (Honey, I would probably have put the ice cream in my *blouse* and not noticed.)

◊

Question:

What's the difference between Noah's Ark and the *Titanic?*
Answer:

An amateur built Noah's Ark. The *Titanic* was built by professionals.

—VIA REV. KARL R. KRAFT, MANTUA, NEW JERSEY

A merry heart hath a continual feast.
—PROVERBS 15:15, KJV

8

Jesus and Reverend Ramsey: Comparative Ministries

❀

Rev. Marvin added some pizzazz to his sermon on TEMPTATION!

© Steve Phelps

FMC member, Rev. J. Christy Ramsey, pastor of Ottawa (Ohio) Presbyterian Church, was asked by his personnel committee to evaluate his ministry in comparison to the ministry of Jesus. Here is Reverend Ramsey's humble response:

Jesus	Pastor Ramsey
Walks on water	Slips on ice
Changes water into wine	Changes water into coffee

Jesus	Pastor Ramsey
Welcomes children	Has children's sermon
Curses fig tree	Kills houseplants
Stills the storm	Puts storm windows in sills
Feeds five-thousand	Buys snacks for youth groups
Sees Nathaniel under far-off tree	Watches world on CNN
Heals centurion's servant at distance	Can use TV remote control
Heals paralyzed man	Gets children to do chores
Raises the dead	Wakes teenagers
Casts out demons	Turns on night-light
Overturns money-changers' tables	Puts away folding tables
Cleanses lepers	Has changed dirty diapers
Light of the world	Turner of light switches
Stands at door and knocks	Has church key
Calls disciples	E-mails session

ANTIDOTES FOR LOW SPIRITS

Some "Antidotes for Low Spirits" recommended in 1820 by Rev. Sydney Smith, an Anglican pastor:

- Go into the shower-bath with a small quantity of water at a temperature low enough to give you a slight sensation of cold— 75° or 80°.
- Read amusing books.
- Be as busy as you can.
- See as much as you can of those friends who respect and like you, and of those acquaintances who amuse you.

- Avoid dramatic representations (except comedy) and serious novels.
- Do good.
- Do as much as you can in the open air without fatigue.
- Make the room where you commonly sit cheerful and pleasant.
- Struggle little by little against idleness.
- Be firm and constant in the exercise of rational religion.

> The joy of the LORD is your strength.
>
> —NEHEMIAH 8:10, NIV

Can You Top These Top Tens?

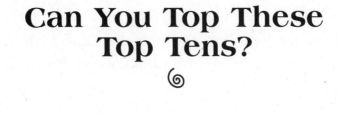

© Ed Sullivan

TOP TEN SIGNS YOU'RE IN A DRY-BONES CHURCH

10. The choir director and the organist quit and no one notices for three months.

9. The baptismal is now being used for chips and dip in the social hall.

8. The pew Bibles donated a year ago still have the cellophane on them.

7. The pastor takes a month-long sabbatical and is told upon his return that his sermons over the last month have been better than ever.

6. The custodian passes away while cleaning the sanctuary, and no one realizes it for three weeks.

5. The pastor has been using the same Scripture passage as his/her text for two months.

4. The pulpit was moved six inches to the left, and twenty-five people volunteer to serve on the task force to investigate.

3. The altar rail has not been cleaned since the custodian passed away.

2. The nursery is being used for long-term storage.

1. Jesus Christ visited and was told he was sitting in someone's seat.

—FMC MEMBER REV. JEFF HANNA, PASTOR OF THE FIRST
UNITED METHODIST CHURCH OF GALION, OHIO.

TOP TEN WAYS TO TELL IF A CHURCH IS SPIRIT-FILLED

10. You have to assign numbers to people who want to share their testimony in worship.

9. As the pastor closes the sermon, the chant of "We want more! We want more!" erupts.

8. The ushers have to empty the collection plates halfway through the offering because they are too full.

7. The choir begins to sing and can't stop.

6. Members begin buying new Bibles because they wore the others out.

5. There is an influx of people asking, "Is there something I can do?"

4. New classes and small groups have to be formed because so many people want to teach.

3. People offer their seats to newcomers.

2. New altar rails have to be installed to handle the crowds.

1. The congregation douses the pastor with a cooler of water at the end of the service.

—REV. JEFF HANNA

TOP TEN REASONS FOR JOINING THE CHURCH CHOIR

10. The collection plate is never passed to the choir.

9. You want to be near the pastor when he preaches in case he says anything heretical.

8. When you forget to do your laundry, the choir robes cover dirty clothes.

7. You want to make sure you always have a seat in church.

6. The chairs in the choir are more comfortable than the chairs in the pews.

5. You can see everyone who is in church and they can see you.

4. The pastor won't see you if you take a short nap.

3. You want to get used to sitting with a group of people in case you're selected for jury duty.

2. Your favorite movie is *The Preacher's Wife*.

1. You'll be the first to know when it's noon because you can see the clock in the rear of the sanctuary.

—VIA REV. H. WARREN CASIDAY, EMANUEL UNITED
CHURCH OF CHRIST, THOMASVILLE, NORTH CAROLINA

You know that you belong to a megachurch when some of the pastors on its staff have never met each other.

© Dik LaPine

TOP TEN EXCUSES FOR NOT ATTENDING CHURCH

Sorry I missed church, but...

10. I can find God in nature.

9. I prefer watching televangelists. (There's just something about a remote control that makes me feel like I'm in control of my own spiritual life.)

8. It would make me miss my Zen class.

7. There are too many hypocrites in church, and besides, it interferes with my tee-time.

6. There's too much hugging and real warmth.

5. There isn't enough hugging and real warmth.

4. I went once, but I didn't recognize the place without the lilies and poinsettias.

3. I'm an atheist—I swear!

2. Even Jesus wouldn't have gone if he'd had to wear pantyhose.

1. The dog ate my offering.

—THE *DISCIPLE*
REPRINTED WITH PERMISSION OF CHRISTIAN BOARD
OF PUBLICATION, ST. LOUIS, MISSOURI, © 1998

Humor is a divine quality, and God has the greatest sense of humor of all. He must have; otherwise He wouldn't have made so many politicians.

—MARTIN LUTHER KING

In Praise of "Ministers of Fun"

© Doc Goodwin

Columnist Paulette Ducharme, OSU, paid tribute to "Ministers of Fun" in a column which is adapted below and is reprinted with permission of Church World, *Maine's Catholic weekly. Ducharme is a retreat director at the Ursuline Residence in Waterville, Maine.*

This article is dedicated to the "Minister of Fun"—that person who is God's wonderful collection of graces and blessings.

The contribution that the Minister of Fun has to give is priceless. In fact, our understanding of salvation depends on it.

The clearest indication that this servant of the Lord is around is usually a spirit of high hilarity, the sound of deep rumbling belly laughs, and a laid-back, kicked-back attitude that says, "God is here; let's celebrate!"

Somehow in the presence of this person, people feel accepted just the way they are, and for some mysterious reason, they are willing to take others the same way.

I think Jesus must have been this kind of person. Why else would people have followed Him for days without even thinking of eating or sleeping?

Children loved Jesus. They ran to Him, crawled all over Him, and probably begged Him for special parables.

These tiniest people, who always start out pure and clear-sighted, could see heaven in His smiling eyes. The sounds of Jesus laughing with the children must have echoed through many sunny afternoons when they all played in the meadows around Nazareth.

He was approachable and made both children and the elderly feel welcome. This is also the hallmark of a Minister of Fun. Children and the elderly can spot them at quite a distance and usually want to be in their close proximity.

Recently, I had the happy occasion to be in the presence of just such a Minister of Fun. (Name withheld to protect the guilty!) I watched as a whole room full of rather sedate ladies was transformed into a dance floor where support hose and varicose veins did things they were never advertised to do.

The sound level went from polite chatter to wild cheers in a matter of minutes once a little lively music got into this Minister of Fun. Corrective lenses were cast off and arthritic bones rattled with mirth as people became more friendly and cheerful.

Hands that regularly only found the strength to knit were clapping with exultation.

People were smiling, laughing, and for that time, seemed happy to be themselves. It was a sacramental moment for me. God was truly present in the midst of a joyful people.

Although there are in our lives times of deep sadness that wound us and weigh down our spirits, they are not what God wants for us. Our hearts are made for happiness. Jesus came that we may have life that is lived to the fullest.

We are sons and daughters of joy. Jesus was the original Minister of Fun because He showed us how to be free from worry and fear. The real seed of God's love is joy!

Not everyone has the God-given gifts or the natural disposition to be a registered Minister of Fun. It is a call that demands a highly developed sense of empathy and a heart that is easily touched by the smallest signs of sadness in others.

We have to have many kinds of people in our lives, and each of their gifts is important to us because they all give us the opportunity to grow somehow.

Yet, in my heart there is a special appreciation for those people who give me a reason to laugh, to enjoy, and to not take myself so seriously. These guardian angels make me conscious of the essence of Christianity, which is basically quite humorous. There is great comedy in the fact that God who is all powerful and great really loves me just the way I am, puny and poor.

Why shouldn't I rejoice? And thankfully, God has provided a whole order of precious people, Ministers of Fun, who can help me do it.

A PRAYER FOR JOY

O everlasting Light, surpassing all created luminaries, flash forth Thy lightning from above, piercing all the most inward parts of my heart. Make clean, make glad, make bright, and make alive my spirit, with all the powers thereof, that I may cleave unto Thee in ecstasies of joy.

—THOMAS À KEMPIS (1380-1471)

WELCOME TO THE '90's

"I'm a worship leader. And you?"

© Steve Phelps

Funereal Humor

"I've heard reports about ministerial burn-out, but this is the first time I've actually seen one."

© Dennis Daniel

TEARS AND LAUGHTER

My dad was an easygoing, laid-back type of guy. So much so that Mom often told him that he would be late for his own funeral.

When Dad passed away, he *was* late for his own wake because of a mix-up between the hospital and the funeral home.

So Mom sat in an office chair at the funeral home and laughed.

We opted to display an empty, closed casket for family and friends at the wake. One gentleman could not understand why the casket was closed.

Unable to avoid his insistent questions, I finally took him aside. "Because it's empty," I whispered.

"Ooooooh!" he said, still nodding his head. "Well, where's your father?"

"He's still at the hospital," I replied.

"Ooooooh!" he said, still nodding his head. "Aren't you rushing things a bit?"

When my Mom passed away, her funeral also had its own little twist. One of her favorite sayings was, "If _____ saw or heard that, they'd roll over in their grave." Well, wouldn't you know that during her funeral, the pallbearers stumbled, causing Mom to roll over onto her side.

Even in the most tragic of circumstances, laughter can ease much of the pain of loss.

My parents, Leo and Rose, have been with Jesus for some time now, but they still manage to make us laugh. May you both rest in the peace, love, joy, and laughter of our Lord.

—FMC MEMBER JAMES J. REYOR SR., SPRINGFIELD, MASSACHUSETTS

Sign in the lobby of a Moscow hotel across from a Russian Orthodox monastery:

"You are welcome to visit the cemetery where famous Russian composers, artists, and writers are buried daily except Thursday."

—VIA PATTY WOOTEN, SANTA CRUZ, CALIFORNIA

Sign in a Pennsylvania cemetery:

"Persons are prohibited from picking flowers from any but their own graves."

—VIA REV. STUART A. SCHLEGEL,
SANTA CRUZ, CALIFORNIA

Sign in a funeral parlor:

"Ask about our layaway plan."

Sign in front of a small rural church cemetery in Tennessee:

"As the maintenance of the church cemetery is becoming increasingly costly, it would be appreciated if those who are willing would clip the grass around their own grave."

—VIA GEORGE GOLDTRAP

Notice in the March 28, 1997, St. Louis Review:

"The men and women of the Catholic Cemeteries wish the blessings of the Risen Christ to all who bury their dead with love and hope in the Resurrection."

Rick Moore of the Crimson River Quartet, Mission Viejo, California, tells this true story:

A southern-gospel group arrived home from a singing tour and was called by the widow of a man in their church who had just passed away. The widow asked them to sing three of her husband's favorite songs at the funeral: "In the Garden," "Amazing Grace," and "Jingle Bells."

The group leader had misgivings about singing "Jingle Bells" at a funeral, but when the widow insisted that her husband loved the song, he agreed to sing it, but told her that they would be singing it "real slow."

At the funeral service, the group sang all three songs, including "Jingle Bells," slowly and mournfully. Afterward, the widow thanked the group for singing, and added: "Oh, I remember the name of the song my husband liked so much. It wasn't 'Jingle Bells'; it was 'When They Ring Those Golden Bells.'"

When comedian Henny Youngman died at the age of 91, hundreds of comics and friends paid tribute to him at his funeral at Riverside Memorial Chapel in Manhattan, the *Bergen Record* reported. Youngman was famous for his rapid-fire one-liners, including "Take my wife...please." After an effusive eulogy, Youngman's rabbi, Noach Valley of the Actor's Temple in New York, added: "Dear God, take Henny Youngman...please."

—BILL HANZALEK, RAMSEY, NEW JERSEY

Laney Penn of Columbia, South Carolina passed on an obituary for a seventy-seven-year-old woman that appeared in the *State* newspaper of Columbia. The obituary reported that graveside services for the woman "will be held at 2 P.M. Friday at Broad River Baptist Church Cemetery, Smyrna."

It then noted that the deceased woman "was a member of Broad River Baptist Church Cemetery."

On a trip to England, FMC member Susan Pellowe of Chicago visited her grandfather's grave in a Cornwall cemetery. She found this epitaph on the nearby tombstone of Samuel Carne, chosen by his widow, a friend of Susan:

He Knew How to Smile

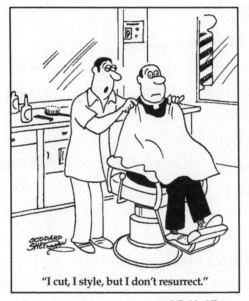

"I cut, I style, but I don't resurrect."

© Goddard Sherman

There once was a deacon from Yuma
Who told a church joke to a puma.
    Now his body lies
    Under hot desert skies.
For the puma had no sense of huma.

—VIA JOSEPH A. MAHER, OXNARD, CALIFORNIA

We've had three funerals in the past ten days. At every funeral I urge people to live life fully and completely. We always say such nice things about the deceased, only good things. So, dear saints, please say those good things about and to the living. Don't wait for a funeral.

—REV. FELIX A. LORENZ, NORTHVILLE, MICHIGAN

AUNT SELMA'S RUNAWAY HEARSE

Aunt Selma became blind after her husband died at age forty. But she could still see the humor in any situation. When people came to see her, she could tell who they were by the tone of their voice; happy, sad, perky, vibrant.

She had been around. She was a waitress in a restaurant in Hollywood, California. Many people would go directly to her because they knew they would be greeted cheerfully and honestly.

After her tours around the country, she moved back to northern Illinois near the church of her childhood in Creston, which is five miles east of Rochelle.

Having been a widow for forty years, she died in her eighties. But she wasn't through laughing yet. After the dignified funeral in the little Creston church, the cars headed for the cemeteries.

I say cemeteries because the mourners just knew she would be buried in Rochelle, where her husband was buried, and the driver of the hearse was just as sure she would be buried with the rest of her family in Creston.

So the mourners went west to the cemetery where her husband was buried, and the driver of the hearse with Aunt Selma went east to the cemetery in Creston.

Her spirit must have laughed so hard it split the air like lightning. The funeral director had to call the highway patrol to catch the runaway hearse. I've heard tremendous laughter at weddings. But never more than at Aunt Selma's funeral. I can still hear her laughing from her lofty perch in a brighter world.

—FMC MEMBER DENNY J. BRAKE, LUTHERAN PASTOR, RALEIGH, NORTH CAROLINA

Rev. John Riley, rector of All Saints Episcopal Church, Jacksonville, Florida, passed on this story:

Following the funeral of a very prominent church person, the family left the church and began to form the funeral procession to the cemetery. The funeral director carefully instructed the parishioners on which car was to follow which car.

A motorcycle escort led about thirty cars to the cemetery. About four blocks from the cemetery's main gate, the driver of the fourth car suddenly decided that he was hungry and wanted to stop off at his nearby home for lunch.

When the driver made a right turn onto his street, twenty-five cars behind him in the procession followed him.

At the graveside, the funeral director, the family of the deceased, and Reverend Riley wondered what had happened to everyone. Due to time limits in the cemetery, the committal was read and the blessing given. It was not until the next day that they discovered that one friend of the deceased had an enormous gathering at his home for lunch.

DEATH AND TAXES

"The point is to get them to render unto the Lord before they find out what they must render unto the IRS."

A priest from Holland was visiting our rectory recently, and one night at dinner he explained that the red, white, and blue in the flag of the Netherlands symbolizes our taxes. We turn red when we talk about them, white when we get our tax bill, and blue when we pay them.

One of the American priests responded, "That's the same with us. But we see stars, too."

—MSGR. CHARLES DOLLEN, *THE PRIEST*

I tried to pay my tax bill with a smile—but they wanted cash.

—VIA JOHN NADEAU, MEDFORD, MASSACHUSETTS

BELIEVE IT OR NOT

During a trip to Stockholm, Sweden, Eduardo Sierra, a Spanish Roman Catholic, stopped to pray at a church. The church was empty except for a coffin with the corpse of a man.

Sierra prayed for the deceased man for twenty minutes. He then signed a condolence book after he saw a note inviting those who prayed for the dead man to enter their names and addresses. He was the first to sign.

Weeks later, Sierra got a call from Stockholm. Jens Svenson, seventy-three, the man in the coffin, turned out to be a real-estate tycoon with no close relatives. In his will, Svenson wrote, "Whoever prays for my soul gets all my belongings."

Sierra is now a millionaire.

—THE *BILD*, HAMBURG, GERMANY

Before Larry J. Crocker became minister of Marbach Christian Church in San Antonio, Texas, he was a funeral director. At one funeral, he recalls, he got his tie caught while closing a casket in front of twelve hundred people. "Needless to say," he says, "the decorum was lost, as was the tie."

Every man should keep a fair-sized cemetery in which to bury the faults of his friends.

—HENRY WARD BEECHER

Heavenly Humor

© Sandy Campbell, Reprinted courtesy of the *Tennessean*, Nashville

The *Tennessean* in Nashville carried this cartoon by Sandy Campbell the day after Red Skelton, the king of the clean clown-comedians, passed away at the age of eighty-four. Comedian Steve Allen commented that he saw "something about Red that was partly the little boy," a quality that made him "a great clown and remarkably funny even in his latter years." Comedian George Goldtrap told *The Joyful Noiseletter* that when Skelton was in Nashville, he was asked why he didn't use four-letter words in his comedy. Skelton replied: "Why should people pay me to say words they can read for free on the bathroom wall?" Skelton once told an AP reporter: "Today's comics use four-letter words as a shortcut to thinking."

© Ed Sullivan

TOP 10 REASONS WHY HEAVEN IS LOOKING GOOD

A cherished friend of FMC member Fred W. Sanford, of Schaumburg, Illinois, battled cancer for years. "Several days before she died," Sanford said, "I thought the gift of humor would lift her up.

"As she lay on her couch with labored breath, I told her I had a list called 'The Top 10 Reasons Why Heaven Is Looking Good' and shared them with her:

10. You can begin the Lord's Prayer "Our Father, who art here..."

9. You can find out the answer to the question, "Why?"

8. Wings.

7. Soul music for eternity.

6. Real golden arches.

5. Great view.

4. "No pain, no gain" becomes "No pain, no pain."

3. When you say, "Oh God…" you'll hear, "What?"

2. Harp lessons.

1. Totally fat free.

—© 1997 Fred W. Sanford. Reprinted with permission.

"You've been waiting 20 years for me and all you can say is 'What's for dinner?'"

© Marty Bucella

Three doctors died, went to heaven, and met St. Peter at the gates. St. Peter asked the first doctor why he thought he deserved to enter.

"I was a doctor with the Christian Medical and Dental Society," the physician replied. "Every year, I went to the Southwest for three weeks and treated the poor Native Americans free-of-charge."

"Welcome," said St. Peter. He asked the second doctor, "And what did you do?"

"I was a missionary in Africa for eleven years, and worked in a hospital helping the tribes there," she replied.

"Enter into the joy of the Lord," St. Peter said. He turned to the third doctor and asked, "What did you do?"

"I was a doctor at an HMO."

"Come on in," St. Peter said, "but you can only stay for three days."

"I'm originally from Australia. How about you?"

© Harley Schwadron

A man died and went to heaven. St. Peter escorted him past mansion after dazzling mansion until they came to a dilapidated shack at the end of the street.

The man was stunned and said, "St. Peter, why am I stuck with a rundown shack when all of these other people have mansions?"

"Well, sir," replied St. Peter, "we did the best we could with the money you sent us."

—RICK MOORE, THE CRIMSON RIVER QUARTET,
MISSION VIEJO, CALIFORNIA

Seen on a bulletin board at Mayo Clinic:

Cancer is limited.

It cannot cripple love.

It cannot shatter hope.

It cannot corrode faith.

It cannot eat away peace.

It cannot destroy confidence.

It cannot kill friendship.

It cannot shut out memories.

It cannot silence courage.

It cannot invade the soul.

It cannot reduce eternal life.

It cannot quench the Spirit.

It cannot lessen the power of the Resurrection.

—AUTHOR UNKNOWN, VIA PENNY MCBRIDE,
DECATUR, ILLINOIS

Researchers say that cheerful people live longer than grouchy people, maybe because the surly bird catches the germ.

—CHARLES MILAZZO, ST. PETERSBURG, FLORIDA

No pessimist ever discovered the secrets of the stars, or sailed to an uncharted land, or opened a new heaven to the human spirit.

—HELEN KELLER

"You'll find your doggie two clouds over."

© Ed Sullivan

The Messages on the Refrigerator Door

"Get more exercise and less potluck suppers."

© Goddard Sherman

The following reflections on dieting were written by Cal Samra, editor of The Joyful Noiseletter.

I confess that I am continually tempted to commit what was once called the sin of gluttony, but which has come to be known in modern times as "snacking."

For most of my life I've been lean and trim, but as the years passed, the girth broadened, and suddenly last spring I was astonished to discover that I was tipping the scales at 187—15 to 20 pounds overweight.

The members of my family kept dropping subtle hints. Every time my two older sons came by for a visit, they would grin and poke/grab/squeeze the tire around my waistline. But when your ten-year-old son starts calling you "chubby," it's time to ask for prayers.

After our family physician advised me that my blood-pressure and cholesterol levels were up, mysterious messages began to appear on our refrigerator door: newspaper and magazine clippings, Scripture passages, etc., attached with magnets.

Now Martin Luther started the Reformation by nailing messages on a church door. But the messages on our refrigerator door were different.

- Headline over an Associated Press story: "More Than Half of Americans Are Overweight."
- "When you are fasting, do not put on a gloomy look as the hypocrites do." (Matthew 6:16, NJB)
- News item from the *Detroit News:* The woman who cooked for Elvis Presley for twenty-six years will appear in a TV documentary titled "The Burger and the King" and will describe the overweight Elvis's voracious eating habits before he died at a comparatively youthful age.
- "Let your moderation be known unto all men." (Philippians 4:5, KJV)
- A clip from an article in *Christianity Today* reporting that a highly respected Christian healer, who had helped thousands of people with his prayers, had allowed himself to

balloon up to 280 pounds, and now was struggling val-
iantly against a heart condition, depression, and cancer.

- A clip from another publication noting that the great English wit and defender of Christianity, G. K. Chesterton, was
an enormous three hundred-plus pounds when he died at
the young age of sixty-two.

- An Associated Press story from Atlanta describing a well-
ness and weight-loss program called First Place, which
started at First Baptist Church in Houston, Texas, and
now operates in about ten thousand churches. One
woman said: "We memorize a Scripture verse and recite
it when we stand on the scales." Carole Lewis, national
director of First Place, explained: "We have people who
know Christ, so spiritually they're OK, but they are out of
balance physically and they have no joy. There are a lot of
Christians who are extremely overweight."

- A *New York Times* article noting that during the six weeks
of Lent, Eastern Orthodox Christians abstain from eating
meat, cheese, butter, milk, and eggs. The article also reported
that the Eastern Orthodox Church for centuries also has
encouraged parishioners to abstain from animal products
every Wednesday and Friday throughout the year.

Who, I wondered, was persecuting me with these refrigerator messages?

Late one night, when I came to bed, I found my wife Rose
reading a cookbook titled *Twelve Months of Monastery Soups* by
Brother Victor-Antoine.

"Listen to this," she said, reading from the book. "John J.
Michnovicz, M.D., president and medical director of the

Foundation for Preventive Oncology, recommends this book, and says, 'Modern science has begun to appreciate the age-old wisdom of a diet focused more on vegetables and less on meat.' From now on we're going to have monastery soups five times a week!"

"Monastery soups?" I exclaimed. "No way!"

"Well, then," she said, "you can try fasting. Jesus prayed *and* fasted."

"Praying comes easy to me," I said, "but fasting is hard. Fasting had to be easier for the early Christians. They didn't live in neighborhoods a stone's throw from a variety of fancy restaurants and fast-food establishments. They weren't assaulted day and night by TV and radio messages saying 'eat...eat...EAT!' And their wives didn't put messages on their refrigerator doors telling them not to snack, because they didn't have refrigerators!"

"Then why don't you get more exercise?" my wife said. "That will help you lose weight."

"I'm going to start working out at the Y," I said. "Before you start cooking monastery soups, let me try that."

For the next seven months, I worked out faithfully, lifting weights in the fitness center at our local YMCA. I played tennis regularly. I bought a bike and rode it every day. I gardened and mowed the lawn. I became a Little League manager.

One day, seven months later, when I stepped on the scales, I weighed in at 186 pounds. I had lost exactly one pound. I felt better, and I was more muscular, but all the exercise had simply redistributed the weight.

When I came to bed that night, I found my wife reading a

book titled *Love Yourself, So Hate the Weight!* by Brother Robert Driscoll of Petersham, Massachusetts, who describes himself as "the Metabolic Monk."

"This monk says he weighed 237 pounds and lost 114 pounds in fourteen months on a vegetarian diet and an exercise program," my wife said cheerfully. "He also suggests that you put two photos of yourself on the refrigerator—one when you were slim and one when you are overweight—to remind yourself of your goal."

The next day at dinnertime, my wife placed a bowl of steaming hot monastery soup in front of me.

"Whataya mean, 'maybe we should give ourselves up during Lent'?"

Last spring, as I was getting ready to go into the city, the church janitor asked if I could stop at a hardware store and get him a vise grip. I had no idea what he really wanted, but I said I'd get it for him.

The clerk at the store turned out to be a parishioner, so I asked him, "Do you have any heavy-duty vise?"

"Sorry, Father," he said, "I gave them all up for Lent."

—MSGR. CHARLES DOLLEN, *THE PRIEST*

The spirit cannot endure the body when overfed, but if underfed, the body cannot endure the spirit.

—FRANCIS DE SALES

DIETER'S PRAYER

The Lord is my shepherd, I shall not want.
He maketh me lie down and do push-ups,
He giveth me sodium-free bread,
He restoreth my waistline,
He leadeth me past the refrigerator for mine own sake.
He maketh me partake of broccoli instead of potatoes,
He leadeth me past the pizzeria.
Yea, though I walk through the bakery
I shall not falter, for Thou art with me;
With diet colas I am comforted.
Thou preparest a diet for me in the presence of my enemies.
Thou anointest my lettuce with low-cal olive oil.

My cup will not overflow.

Surely Ry-Krisp and D-Zerta shall follow me all the days of
my life,

And I shall live with the pangs of hunger forever.

Amen

—Author unknown

❏
❏
◊

Exercise is the cheapest, most readily available, and most effective antidepressant. Exercise elevates endorphin levels. Endorphins are powerful natural mood elevators. A brisk twenty-to-thirty minute walk three times a week may be what you need to lift your depression.

—Julian Whitaker, M.D.,
Newport Beach, California

Three Cheers for the Big, Beautiful, and Benevolent

*FMC member Inez Lawson, a freelance writer in Bowling Green,
Missouri, contributed the following:*

My doctor had raised, once again, the need for me to lose weight. "Lord," I grumbled as I drove home from the doctor's office, "I'm fed up with diets, dieting, and diet-watching. All this blah, blah, blah about body weight is driving me to a bigger appetite."

Being thin is not the purpose of living life. Everybody wasn't meant to fit into a size five, seven, or nine.

Just the thought of eating celery, radishes, and lettuce for weeks is enough to raise my blood pressure.

This world didn't get to be almost civilized and pretty much messed up by just thin people. Large, hefty, and stout folks have been out there too, clearing land, constructing buildings, paving highways. I've also noticed that some of the world's nastiest people, criminals, and movie monsters are skinny.

While I was fixing myself a salad in the kitchen of my home, suddenly I heard my neighbor Verna's voice vault across the driveway through my open window. She was calling urgently.

I looked out and saw Verna standing with her back to her garage door and her hands holding the front hood of her large sedan. Now she was yelling desperately.

I ran out behind her car and it seemed that Verna was straining to hold on to her car to keep it from rolling backward down the inclining driveway and smashing a car parked across the street. I tried to help her by pushing against the driver's side.

Verna began to shriek. "Turn the engine off! Hurry!"

I managed to open the door and found the keys in the ignition. The motor jolted to a stop, but the car rolled backward.

"Use the emergency brake!" she shouted. I found it and finally stopped the car.

"What on earth happened?" I asked Verna.

"Thank God you heard me!" she gasped. "I left the car running and stepped out to raise the garage door. I heard a loud thump. The gearshift jumped into drive, and the car pinned me against the garage door. It could have crushed me, but on the brighter side, it only squeezed a couple of ounces off me."

Back at home, it pleased me to consider that two svelte, slender, skinny women couldn't have handled that runaway car. But two big, beautiful, benevolent women did it. And lived to tell about it.

Verna is a large woman who is warm, generous, loving, and always willing to help, lend support, or give of herself. In size and in spirit, she is big, beautiful, and benevolent.

There are a lot of big-hearted, big-minded, big people in this world, and whatever their sins at the table might be, I think the Lord will be kind to them in the end because they are big-hearted.

© Ed Sullivan

Not even the Lenten season can prevent *The Joyful Noise-letter* from making its appointed rounds.

—DAVID BRIGGS, THE ASSOCIATED PRESS

Christ Is Risen! Smile!

"Well, I guess this leaves only taxes as being for certain."

EASTER HUMOR

Lawrence W. Althouse, a retired United Methodist pastor in Dallas who writes a syndicated newspaper column, tells this story:

"Many years ago, when I was working in a suburban New York church, I was asked to take part in an ecumenical Easter dawn pageant held at the Bronx River Parkway. At 5:15 A.M. I was zipping down the parkway. But within moments, the flashing red lights of a police car pulled me over.

"I was in the costume of an angel — complete with wings and halo. When the officer walked toward me and looked in the window, I thought his eyes were going to pop out of his head.

"He regained his composure and asked, 'Do you have any idea how fast you were going?'

"I told him I didn't, but I really had to hurry because 'I've got to get to the resurrection on time.'

"The officer stared at me, his face clouded over, and he blurted out: 'Go! Just go!' And I did."

—FROM "THE BIBLE SPEAKS" COMMUNITY PRESS
SERVICE, FRANKFORT, KENTUCKY

From the April 1997 bulletin of Spring Arbor (Michigan) Free Methodist Church:

"7:00 A.M. Easter Sunrise Service. Led by persons in the cemetery. Followed by juice and donuts in the fellowship hall."

—VIA RENEE RUNYON, SPRING ARBOR, MICHIGAN

One Easter Sunday morning, the rector, Rev. Tom Bowers, was preaching a children's sermon at Saint Bartholomew's Episcopal Church, next door to the Waldorf-Astoria Hotel on New York City's fancy Park Avenue. Bowers was using a paper bag filled with props.

At one point, he pulled an egg from the bag, and pointing to the egg, asked the children, "What's in here?"

"I know!" a little boy exclaimed. "Pantyhose!"

—ANDY FISHER, DENVILLE, NEW JERSEY

On Easter Sunday, a Sunday school teacher at the Church of Christ in Old Hickory, Tennessee, gave each of her children twelve eggs and helped them paint the name of each of the twelve apostles on their eggs. Her intent was to teach the children the names of the apostles.

Four-year-old Leah, granddaughter of George and Peggy Goldtrap, brought her eggs home but forgot to take them into the house.

Leah's father found her searching in the family station wagon. "What are you looking for?" he asked.

"I'm looking for my twelve opossums," she replied.

Our four-year-old daughter sometimes joins us in singing hymns in church. On the way home after the Easter service, she suddenly began singing, "Up from the gravy a rose." ("Up from the grave he arose.")

—CHRIS GOOD

During an Easter service, as the pastor and the choir processed silently down the aisle carrying lighted candles, a small preschool boy became excited and burst out singing, "Happy birthday to you."

—REV. VERNON BABCOCK, HUNTER COMMUNITY
CHURCH, FRANKLIN, OHIO

At the dinner table, three-year-old Maria Bridgeman, daughter of Paul and Gina Bridgeman of Scottsdale, Arizona, was telling the family what she had learned that day in Sunday school at

La Casa de Cristo Lutheran Church in Scottsdale, Arizona.

"A story about Laz'rus," Maria said.

"And what happened to Lazarus?" her brother Ross, nine, asked her.

"Well, he was dead, and Jesus went to see him," she replied.

"And then what happened?" Ross asked.

After a pause, Maria answered, "Jesus held up his hand and yelled, 'On your mark, get set, go Lazarus!'"

TALE OF THE EASTER CAT

My husband, Don, comes from a long, long line of "cats-as-pets" haters, and he was always adamant about how he was never going to have a cat in *his* house.

Whenever my dad, Carl, heard my husband say that, Dad would laugh, remembering the times when he, too, had said the same thing so emphatically.

Then Dad would tell my husband about the time—when I was eight years old— a cat arrived on our doorstep just minutes before a blizzard. My Mom and I convinced him it would be cruel and unusual punishment to throw the cat out into the storm.

So he allowed us to make a bed in the garage until the storm was over. But when the blizzard stopped, we found that we had one cat and eight kittens!

My dad said, "Okay, you can keep them, but only until the kittens are weaned." But by then, the mama cat had gained a reputation for clearing the house and shed of mice, so she stayed on for six more years through her old age.

My dad would always tell my husband that there would come a time when the same thing would happen to him. "No way!" my husband declared, even though our daughter, Angela, really wanted a cat.

One year late in March, between Palm Sunday and Easter Sunday, Dad died suddenly, just as he wanted—active on a golf course, having just shot a hole-in-one!

Four hours after we came home from the funeral, a cat firmly planted itself on our doorstep. When Angela saw the cat, she cried out joyfully: "Grandpa sent me a kitty as an Easter present!"

Even though we didn't encourage the cat or feed it for several days, it refused to leave. Finally, my husband gave in and let Angela keep the cat.

It would be just like Dad, I thought, to send Angela that cat as his parting gift. So my Dad had the last laugh after all!

—FMC MEMBER CINDY H. MELANCON, AMARILLO, TEXAS, EDITOR OF *CONVERSATIONS*, A MONTHLY NEWSLETTER FOR WOMEN FIGHTING OVARIAN CANCER

© Steve Phelps

A Sunday school teacher asked her class about the meaning of Easter. A little boy raised his hand and said: "That's when we shoot off firecrackers and celebrate our freedoms."

A little girl said, "No, that's when we eat the turkey and give thanks."

"I know!" a third youngster exclaimed. "That's when Jesus comes out of the tomb—but if he sees his shadow, he goes back in."

—VIA FR. HARRY WINTER, OMI, DIRECTOR OBLATE
CENTER FOR MISSION STUDIES, WASHINGTON, D.C.

A small boy ran home and excitedly told his parents: "School will be dismissed for good on Friday, March 28!"

"I just don't believe that," his mother said.

"It's true," the boy said. "I just got this note from the teacher."

The teacher's note said: "School will be dismissed at 11 A.M. for Good Friday, March 28."

—GEORGE GOLDTRAP

You might be a preacher if you've ever wanted to wish people "Merry Christmas" at Easter because that'll be the next time you'll see them.

—FROM STAN TOLER, YOU MIGHT BE A PREACHER IF...

WHY CAN'T SOMEONE INVENT AN "EASTER GRASS CATCHER"?

Once again, people all across the nation will be waging war on those elusive, green creatures that invade our homes every year around this time. They stick to our clothing, bury themselves in the carpeting, and cling to our household pets. Though they have no wings, they take flight when chased by a broom and, just when you think you've seen the last of them, you find another one!

I'm talking about Easter grass—those light, wispy strands of artificial turf that serve as bedding for the chocolate bunnies, marshmallow chicks, and colored eggs found in our children's baskets every Easter. Now, these hard-to-get-rid-of little rascals even come in pink and yellow, adding some color to our frustration.

Some years ago, I decided to try and conquer the little beasts by competing with myself from year to year. The object was to see how many days sooner than the previous year I could wipe out the very last strand! In 1993, the last one was found ninety-seven days after Easter when I tried to slip into an old pair of shoes.

In 1994, I cut eleven days off that number when I discovered the last green meanie under the vegetable drawer in the refrigerator.

Then, last year, I felt very proud when I eliminated what I thought was the last of it only sixty-eight days after Easter! But, alas! When we moved the couch to put up the Christmas tree, there it was: Easter grass—one nasty little strand of it that seemed to be glaring up at me as if to say, "Aha! So you thought you were rid of me, did you?"

Now I ask you, if the great inventors of this country can make metal detectors so people can roam the beaches collecting aluminum pop tops, and magic wands for picking up bingo markers, why can't someone invent an Easter grass catcher?

As for me, I admit defeat. From here on in, I've sworn to use shredded newspaper. It's much easier to clean up and, after all, it's good enough for real rabbits.

—SANDY TOBIN, CLEARWATER, FLORIDA

Easter is the New Year's Day of the soul.

—A. B. SIMPSON

An Easter Parable for Preachers and Theologians

Sean Gonsalves, a reporter for the Cape Cod Times, *Hyannis, Massachusetts, writes a regular nationally syndicated column. This column by Gonsalves appeared at Easter time. (Dist. by Universal Press Syndicate. Reprinted with permission. All rights reserved.)*

Growing up, I spent more than a few Sundays at Cornerstone Missionary Baptist Church in East Oakland. From time to time

I am deluged with a flood of memories of that blessed place off MacArthur Boulevard.

A good number of those memories were provided by the church mothers, their prayers, and occasional advice. "Jesus said the kingdom of God is inside of us. So we ought to leave a little heaven behind everywhere we go. Put a smile on that face, young man."

I celebrated Easter with 1.5 billion other Christian brothers and sisters across the globe. It's around this time of year that one of the most vivid of my church recollections flashes in front of my mind's eye over and over again.

The preacher (whose name I cannot recall) had just given a powerful message about how the human spirit can be perpetually renewed by God's spirit. It was a magnificent display of the oratorical genius that has long been a part of the Afro-Christian tradition—the rhythmic cadences, the lucid and lyrical language, punctuated with anecdotes that highlight the tragi-comedy of everyday life.

"I am going to end this morning by telling you something that happened when I was in seminary," he said, dabbing his forehead with a white handkerchief that had been folded into a perfect square.

"I went to the University of Chicago Divinity School. Every year they used to have what was called 'Baptist Day.' It was a day when they invited the entire Baptist community in the area to visit the school, basically because they wanted the Baptist dollars to keep coming in," he explained.

"On this day everyone was to bring a bag lunch to be eaten

outdoors in a grassy picnic area giving the students, faculty, and visitors a chance to mingle.

"And every 'Baptist Day' the school would invite one of the greatest minds in theological education to give a lecture. This one year the great Paul Tillich came to speak."

The preacher paused to sip some water.

"Dr. Tillich spoke for two and a half hours, proving that the historical Resurrection was false. He quoted scholar after scholar and book after book, concluding that since there was no such thing as the historical Resurrection, the African-American religious tradition was groundless, emotional mumbo-jumbo, because it was based on a relationship with Jesus, who, in fact, never rose from the dead in any literal sense."

The preacher told us that Dr. Tillich ended his talk with a sweeping, "Are there any questions?"

The silence in the packed lecture hall was deafening.

Then, finally, after about thirty seconds—it seemed like five minutes—an old, dark-skinned preacher with a head full of short-cropped woolly white hair stood up in the back of the auditorium.

"Docta Tillich, I got a question," he said as all eyes turned toward him. He reached into his bag lunch and pulled out an apple.

"Docta Tillich..." Crunch, Munch, Munch, Munch...

"Now, I ain't never read them books you read..." Crunch, Munch, Munch, Munch... "and I can't recite the Scriptures in the original Greek...Crunch, Munch, Munch, Munch... "I don't know nothin' about Niebuhr and Heidegger..." Crunch, Munch, Munch, Munch...

He finished the apple. Then he began to lick his fingertips and pick his teeth.

"All I wanna know is: This apple I just ate—was it bitter or sweet?"

Dr. Tillich paused for a moment and answered in exemplary scholarly fashion: "I cannot possibly answer that question, for I haven't tasted your apple."

The white-haired preacher dropped the core of his apple into his crumpled paper bag, looked up at Dr. Tillich, and said calmly, "Neither have you tasted my Jesus."

The one-thousand-plus in attendance could not contain themselves.

The auditorium erupted with roaring laughter, cheers, and applause. Paul Tillich promptly thanked his audience and left the lectern.

Looking on the bright side won't hurt your eyes.

—Rev. Denny J. Brake, Raleigh, North Carolina

Does a Happy Jesus Make You Sad?

THE RISEN CHRIST BY THE SEA

Rev. Paul Mueller of Bowling Green, Ohio, is a columnist for the Catholic Chronicle *of Toledo. The following excerpts are from Fr. Mueller's Easter column, which appeared along with a print of* The Risen Christ by the Sea. *Many churches—Protestant and*

Catholic—have seen The Risen Christ by the Sea *as a representa-tion of "the Easter Laugh"—God's last laugh on the devil—and have inserted it in their Easter Sunday bulletins. Full-color prints in various sizes are available from the Fellowship of Merry Christians.*

I have a large print of Jack Jewell's *The Risen Christ by the Sea*. It is a full-color painting of a joyful, risen Jesus appearing to His disciples.

I fantasize Jesus saying to His stunned followers, "Hey guys, I told you I'd be rising from the tomb. Let's go fishing."

I have been using this painting at my parish missions to depict Christ's victory over sin and death. Most people like the idea of a happy Jesus, but some folks think it is sacrilegious to represent Jesus as happy. "Jesus isn't happy; He's sad and He's crying," one irate person wrote me anonymously.

I remember we had statues and "holy pictures" on our walls at home. Almost every Catholic home had a large framed picture of the Sacred Heart of Jesus and Mary, the Last Supper, Gethsemane, and a very realistic depiction of Jesus wearing the crown of thorns.

Besides the occasional Good Shepherd and Christ with the little children, there weren't many representations of a smiling or joyful Jesus.

I have noticed, too, that in the recent rash of claimed apparitions of Jesus or Mary the two are invariably sad, crying, or issuing dire warnings. Never do they smile and encourage and commend all the good people in the world.

Fr. Richard Rohr said that half of life is pure pain, the cross, and half is pure joy, the resurrection. That means that when either half is missing, we are missing half the message.

A teacher told me that when you have a class of children draw a picture of the crucifixion, half of the students will put a smile on the face of Jesus. That's a pretty good way to look at our lives.

Besides the smiling Jesus, I have a large crucifix on my bedroom wall. Jesus spent a lot of blood and tears to show us that our Good Fridays can lead to happy Easters, that "through our tears we can look joyfully to resurrection."

The disciples were filled with joy at seeing the [risen] Lord.

—JOHN 20:20, NJB

In Which of These Faces Would a Pipe Look Good?

"We have spotted the pastor's white bronco going along U.S. 53 in the left lane. He's trying to get away on vacation, but we will keep you abreast of his whereabouts. This is Dick Seagull in Jet Copter Six for WDID's Eye on Traffic Report."

© Dik LaPine

The following story is adapted from Charlie W. Shedd, Brush of an Angel's Wing, *published by Servant Publications, Ann Arbor, Michigan (© 1994 Charlie W. Shedd). Used by permission.*

One of the most fascinating attractions on Jekyll Island, Georgia, is the "Faces of Christ" room at the Jekyll Community Presbyterian Church.

Do you ever wonder, "What did Jesus *really* look like?" We know that nobody knows for sure. Yet you'll enjoy the possibilities if you sit in this quiet room and ponder the faces.

Here is the laughing Christ and one who looks like a Notre Dame fullback. The one over here in overalls and that one in a business suit. A black Jesus, an Indian Jesus, an Asian Jesus, all there for your musing. Drawings and paintings, sculpted stone and metal, carvings from wood…they'll stretch your mind and your soul.

I know what that collection can do to the human heart because I collected it, with the help of my congregation, when I was a young pastor in Houston, Texas.

Each day as I looked up at the walls of my study, I would see those faces of Jesus looking at me. Then gradually each picture seemed to take on its own particular character trait. Honesty. Tenderness. Courage. Good cheer. Love. Patience. Mercy. Sacrifice. Commitment. Renunciation. These last three finally did my pipes in.

One of my favorite diversions during those days was smoking a pipe. And the pipe smokers in my congregation kept me well-supplied with new pipes, plus their favorite tobacco.

One day as I was studying my faces of Jesus pictures, it happened. I heard that voice from the inner chamber again. *"In which of these faces would a pipe look good?"*

From that moment I seemed to know my pipes had to go.

But not right away.

For several summers we'd been spending our vacation at Playmore Beach, Rocky Mount, a quiet little resort for families on the Lake of the Ozarks. Now there we were again and, as usual, I'd brought my pipes along.

I told the Lord, "I really have quit, you know. But this is vacation, isn't it? Far from the Faces of Jesus collection, far from the youth groups and all those I might influence. What's wrong with a dreamy pipeful up here?"

I got out my pipe box and handled my pipes one by one. "The Whisper" said, *"Hand them over!"*

You know what happened. The Lord and I had it out. Once and for all we settled it. His way.

On the appointed morning, I took up my pipe box, my beloved pipe box, and I rowed out to the middle of the lake. At least a half-mile from our cabin, I lifted the box gently and dropped it over the side of the boat. "Good-bye, you poor dears. This I am doing for the Lord, and this is farewell forever. May you rest in peace."

Only they didn't.

The next morning where do you suppose my pipes were? *They had washed up on our very beach, right there in front of our cabin!*

One hundred cabins where they could have settled. Or was it two hundred? One-half mile they'd traveled. Or was it several miles bouncing on the lake before they decided to come home?

You can imagine the long talks we had that day, my wife Martha and I. She knew I loved my pipes and how much I wanted to keep them. She liked them too. They made her think of her father. Now I argued again. Couldn't I keep them at least as souvenirs of an unbelievable happening? Might I have possibly made the wrong decision? Had I been unduly pious about my faces of Jesus?

Over and over I argued, but always back to the same cruel words—Renunciation. Surrender. Commitment.

The next morning, while it was barely day, I rowed back to the middle of the lake—Martha with me this time, to hold my hand. With the other hand, one by one I took each pipe, dropped that particular old friend overboard, and watched it sink to the bottom of the lake.

"There you are, Lord. This time they're yours."

The faces of Christ had done their work.

Forever, this is His call to us: *All I want is all of you for all of Me.*

"We should come back at low tide so you can really appreciate the land I donated to the church."

© Steve Phelps

For health and the constant enjoyment of life, give me a keen and ever-present sense of humor; it is the next best thing to an abiding faith in Providence.

—GEORGE B. CHEEVER

Have a Merry Mother's Day!

"I hate it when Mom refers to this as the 'miracle of the loafers and the dishes.'"

© Ed Sullivan

A FLOOD OF BLESSINGS

FMC member William C. McVeigh and his wife, Ruth, who live in Fountain Hills, Arizona, have fourteen children. He tells this story about their own "flood experience":

Back in September 1951, we were living in an old house in Jackson, Michigan, and Ruth was expecting our ninth child. The plumbing quite often sprung a leak, but the leaks could usually be easily fixed by wrapping cotton string over the spot and painting with the residue at the bottom of a can of lead-based paint.

I had just finished fixing a couple of leaks and was upstairs changing clothes when one of my daughters rushed up and told me the water burst. I dashed down to the basement, expecting to see water gushing from the spots I had repaired. I was relieved to find that all was well.

I went back to the kitchen, where Ruth and the kids were gathered and assured them that everything was okay.

Ruth said: "*My* water broke."

After a hurried trip to the hospital, son Joseph was born three hours later.

Our next five births were crisis-free. But three of our sons—Robert, Charles, and James (the fourteenth child)—were all born on December 4 in different years.

On each December 4 thereafter, Ruth made one birthday cake. We'd sing to Bobby; remove four candles and sing to Charlie; then remove three candles and sing to Jimmy.

As Ruth and I approach our fifty-seventh anniversary, we realize that we have had many blessings bestowed and thank God every day.

JUMP FOR JOY WITH THESE JUMP-ROPE JINGLES

Poet/humorist Dona Maddux Cooper has been married for many years to humorist Dr. Don Cooper, longtime team physician at Oklahoma State University in Stillwater, Oklahoma. She is the author of *Family Ties,* a whimsical collection of poems about her life as a wife, mother, and grandmother.

Not long ago, her Presbyterian church school primary teachers asked her to write some jump-rope jingles. They suggested that the jingles might help the youngsters with Bible knowledge when they said them while jumping rope.

Dona came up with these jump-rope jingles, which adults also might want to try (all you need is a jump rope):

Jesus loves me
This I know
Jump for joy
Jump for joy
For the Bible
Tells me so
Jump for joy
Jump for joy
Loves my dad
Loves my mother
Jump for joy
Jump for joy

Loves my sister
And my brother
Jump for joy
Jump for joy
Loves my neighbor
Loves my teacher
Jump for joy
Jump for joy
Loves my doctor
And my preacher

Jump for joy
Jump for joy
For Jesus.

◇

Adam, Adam, tell me true
What did God tell Eve to do?
God said, "Let that apple be
That is growing on the tree."

◇

Moses, Moses, could I ask it,
Who found you there in the basket?
"I was found by the Pharaoh's daughter,
In the reeds in the shallow water."

◇

Noah, Noah, tell me why
God put a rainbow in the sky?
"To promise that no more would He
flood the land from sea to sea."

◇

Jonah, Jonah will you tell
How it was inside that whale?
"Dark and scary, there's no doubt
I was glad he spit me out."

◇

David, David, brave and true
As a boy what did you do?
"I took my slingshot and a stone
And fought Goliath all alone."

MOTHER'S DAY MEDITATIONS

The greatest teacher I ever had was my mother.

—GEORGE WASHINGTON

All that I am and all that I ever hope to be, I owe to my mother.

—ABRAHAM LINCOLN

Mothers write on the hearts of their children what the world's rough hands cannot erase.

—VIA REV. ROBERT E. HARRIS, ASHEVILLE,
NORTH CAROLINA

An elderly woman in a nursing home declined her pastor's suggestion that she get a hearing aid. "At ninety-one, I've heard enough," she said.

—VIA CATHERINE HALL, PITTSBURGH, PENNSYLVANIA

Just when a mother thinks her job is done, she becomes a grand-mother.

—VIA CATHERINE HALL

Every day has moments of pure joy, even on the dullest and saddest day.

—ANNE MORROW LINDBERGH

The fourth Sunday in Lent—Laetare—was the first Mother's Day, according to Pastor Gary W. Cowall of Saron Lutheran Church in St. Joseph, Michigan. The fourth Sunday in Lent is also called "Mothering Sunday." In England, says Cowall, it was customary for people to bake and present their mothers with a "mothering cake" on the fourth Sunday in Lent.

Only if we are secure in our beliefs can we see the comical side of the universe.

—FLANNERY O'CONNOR

© Steve Phelps

A Nonsoccer Dad Finds Happiness in T-Ball

"If the East 13th Street Klisky Bagel Shop Tigers don't win tomorrow, we're going to be sorely disappointed in you."

© Ed Sullivan

Tim Wildmon of Tupelo, Mississippi, is co-host of Today's Issues, *a nationally syndicated radio show on American Family Radio. This article is adapted from Wildmon's book* I Wonder What Noah Did with the Woodpeckers *(Barbour Publishing, Inc., P.O. Box 719, Uhrichsville, OH 44683. © 1998 Tim Wildmon. Reprinted with permission.)*

My oldest son, Wesley, is five at this writing and much to his dad's pleasure, is beginning to show an interest in sports. But after we watched a soccer match one afternoon, he said, "Dad, soccer just isn't my bag."

"Son, that's all right," I said as I bent down on one knee, placed my hands on Wesley's shoulders, and looked him squarely in the eye.

"Listen to me, Wes, and I'll tell you what my dad told me and what his dad told him:

"We're Americans, Wes. Real, red-blooded, hamburger-eatin', stick-your-own-worm-on-the-hook Americans, and we don't believe in sports where you can't use your hands. If a man can't use his hands, the game ain't worth playin', son. Always remember your daddy told you that."

You have to be careful what you tell kids. Wesley started telling all his friends they were wimps for playing soccer. "My dad said you were against America," Wesley preached to the soccer kids. And their parents got mad at me! Can you believe it? Some people are so touchy when it comes to their kids.

Anyway, he decided to try Little League T-ball. And I decided to manage his T-ball team.

Now I had had considerable experience as a manager in church-league softball. My managerial record in three years was matchless. In 1992, 1993, and 1994, my church softball teams hadn't won a single game.

My guys were the Bad News Bears twenty years older, completely inept.

My pastor once told me, "Tim, I'm sorry to bring this up, but word is getting around town how bad your softball team is and quite frankly, you're killing church visitations."

He strongly suggested that I disband the team and said the

church would even pick up the costs of our shirts so that they could be burned.

I resigned as manager. And the church softball team did win a few games after that.

When I took my managerial talents into Little League T-ball the following season, I discovered that none of my twelve kids (five- and six-year-olds) had a shred of experience in baseball.

At our first game, one of my batters hit the ball and ran as fast as he could—to third base. It reminded me that even in the Christian life, we often spend a lot of energy going in the wrong direction, even with the best intentions. We don't always stop and listen to the Coach.

It was an entertaining two months of T-ball. I had a blast, and so did the kids.

So if God closes the door on you as a church-league softball manager, take heart—He might open it to you as a T-ball manager.

"We're looking for a new board member who can handle a 35% increase in budget, but we'd settle for someone who can play second base on our softball team."

© Steve Phelps

The story was told about a Buddhist Zen master who went up to a hot-dog vendor at a baseball game and said: "Make me one with everything."

Patty Wooten of Santa Cruz, California, adds a new twist to the story. When the Zen master paid with a twenty-dollar bill, the hot-dog vendor put the bill in the cash drawer.

"Where's my change?" the Zen master asked.

"Change must come from within," the hot-dog vendor replied.

FMC member Bruce Burnside of Rockville, Maryland, an ardent fan of the Baltimore Orioles, is forever searching the Bible for references to baseball. He found this reference recently in Ezekiel 45:11 (RSV): "The homer shall be the standard measure." In biblical times, Burnside says, "homer" (pronounced "omer") was a dry measure similar to a bushel.

FATHER'S DAY REFLECTIONS

An important spiritual lesson my father taught me was the value of laughter. His sense of humor was infectious, spreading like wildfire through our home and into the neighborhood, job, church, town, and even casual acquaintances. I'm trying to bring that same kind of joy into my home.

—BILL BUTTERWORTH

There are more collect calls on Father's Day than on any other day of the year, according to Rev. Brian Cavanaugh of Steubenville, Ohio.

Every father should remember that one day his children will follow his example instead of his advice.

—VIA REV. ROBERT E. HARRIS, ASHEVILLE,
NORTH CAROLINA

FOOTNOTES

Every Saturday night, while he watched the news

He would line up four pairs of Sunday School shoes.

There were red T-straps for two little girls.

(One with a ponytail; one with curls.)

There were brown loafers for a freckled-faced boy,

And white high tops for his youngest joy.

He would polish and buff them until they shone—

For these precious children he called his own.

And after the final in-season scores,

He'd turn off the TV; lock all the doors.

Then putting each pair at the foot of each bed,

He would bend down to kiss every sleepyhead,

And silently pray that they would choose

To always walk with God in their polished shoes.

—DONA MADDUX COOPER, *FAMILY TIES*,
STILLWATER, OKLAHOMA

INTERDEPENDENCE DAY

Independence is great! We all want independence. We want to see our children grow to become independent of us. We celebrate our nation's independence on July 4.

Yet there is another side we must learn if we are to be truly free. The signers of the Declaration of Independence discovered their strength by depending on one another. We gain freedom when we learn to depend on others for the help we need.

We discover true freedom when we learn to be interdependent. The words "one another" are found in over a hundred verses in the New Testament. Every Sunday in church is Interdependence Day.

—REV. STANLEY HAGEMEYER, SARANAC (MICHIGAN) COMMUNITY CHURCH

"How did you find out all that neat stuff about my Dad?"

© Wendell W. Simons

A group of pastors were discussing on CNN how wonderful it is to have freedom of religion in America. Evangelist Jerry Falwell said that freedom of religion meant that in America the Pentecostals, if they wanted to, could jump over the pews, and that the Baptists, if they wanted to, could sleep in the pews.

—VIA GEORGE GOLDTRAP

ON BEING A COFFEE MUG FATHER

Several years ago, our kids gave me a colorful coffee mug on which are listed some of the likely contributions of fatherhood—"provider, chauffeur, coach, peacemaker, helping hand, miracle worker, and friend."

Though I drink from the mug each morning, I must confess that I don't often read or reflect on the words, and, let's face it, not all of them represent my particular contributions.

However, they serve as a reminder of just how important the position of a good father can be. The list of ills of a fatherless society is, indeed, very long.

More valuable and somewhat smarter than a mule, a man will learn and play the part of fatherhood. He will never receive an Academy Award, but he will know he made a difference.

—REV. JOHN L. WALLACE, PRESBYTERIAN CHURCH OF
SWEET HOLLOW, MELVILLE, NEW YORK

The Sports Section

"He says that if we can distribute the food to the 5000, then He might let us cater a Promise Keeper's conference."

© Dik LaPine

A GOLFER'S PSALM

Jim Reed of Cotter, Arkansas, author of The Funny Side of Golf, *passed on the following "A Golfer's Psalm," which appeared in Charles Allbright's column in the* Arkansas Democratic-Gazette:

> My golf clubs are mine iniquity;
> I shall not want them anymore.
> My driver maketh my ball to slice into green pastures;
> My brassie causeth it to sink into still waters.

Yea, though I cross the creek in 9,

I dubbeth my approach,

My putt runneth over;

My ball is ever near me;

Its presence confoundeth me.

My clubs and my balls maketh me to prepare
a feast for mine opponents.

Verily, I am their meal ticket.

Surely, I will swing my clubs,

Cussing them, all the days of my life.

And I shall shooteth over 100 forever.

"You would think that up here, on the last
hole, they would let you keep the ball."

© Harley L. Schwadron

A solemn friend of my grandfather used to go for walks on
Sunday, carrying a prayer book, without the least intention of

going to church. And he calmly defended it by saying, "I do it, Chessie, as an example to others."

Few modern men, however false, would dare to be so brazen. And I am not sure he was not really a more genuine fellow than the modern man who says vaguely that he has doubts or hates sermons, when he only wants to go and play golf.

—G. K. Chesterton

After hearing several boasting fishermen stretch the truth about their catches, a mother reminded her son that it's a sin to tell a lie.

On his next fishing trip with his father, the boy asked, "Dad, have you ever lied?"

"Well, yes, I'm afraid I have," his father confessed.

"How about Mother?"

"On occasion, if she felt the truth would hurt, I guess she lied," the father said.

"How about Grandpa and Grandma?"

"I suppose they're like the rest of us," the father said.

"Well," the boy said, "all I can say is, it must be lonesome up in heaven with nobody but God and George Washington!"

—Jim Reed, *The Funny Side of Fishing*

Boxer George Foreman commenting about a heavyweight challenger who was quickly dispatched in the third round: "He made the sign of the cross so often coming into the ring, people thought it was a funeral."

FOOTBALL CHRISTIANITY

Draft choice: Selection of a seat near a church door.

Draw play: What many children and some adults do with their bulletins.

Fumble: Dropping a hymnal or singing the wrong verse.

Sudden death: The pastor who preaches past noon.

Backfield in motion: People who make two or three trips out of the church during the sermon.

Stay in the pocket: What happens to a lot of the money that should go to the church or the missions.

Quarterback sneak: People who quietly exit immediately after communion.

Blitz: The stampede for the door after church.

—VIA FR. ROBERT CONSANI, KALAMAZOO, MICHIGAN

"Do me a favor. Next time we go up to the lake, don't pray to St. Peter the Fisherman."

© Ed Sullivan

The old pastor just couldn't get the knack of programming his VCR. One evening was particularly vexing because he wanted to record an important football game that was on during the parish-council meeting.

The next morning, his young assistant pastor gave him another demonstration and said very patiently: "You have to move the cursor to this particular place."

"What's a cursor?" asked the old pastor suspiciously.

"That's what you were last night when you tried to program this thing," his assistant replied.

—MSGR. CHARLES DOLLEN, *THE PRIEST*

Donald L. Cooper, M.D., team physician to the Oklahoma State University football and basketball teams, is easily recognizable around Stillwater, Oklahoma. Dr. Cooper drives around town in a car with the license plate: "JOC DOC."

© Harley L. Schwadron

COACHES GO BACK TO THE BIBLE

Coaching was around way back in biblical times. I'm quite sure there was a coach yelling at Goliath not to take David lightly, no matter what the point spread was; and after David pulled the upset, Goliath's coach said on his coach's show that somehow Goliath came out flat.

Frankly, I don't know why anyone would want to coach. Here's a glimpse at a coach's daily schedule:

- 6:08 A.M.: Wake up, turn on radio, hear callers calmly suggest that you are a worthless dirtbag.
- 6:17 A.M.: Get updated player arrest total.
- 7:02 A.M. to 6:45 P.M.: Practice, watch film.
- 6:46 P.M.: Go potty.
- 6:49 P.M. to 11:13 P.M.: Film, meetings, have secretary call home for update (such as recent births or deaths of key family members).
- ll:27 P.M.: Turn on sportscast, watch 113th replay of fumble, sob softly to sleep.

—BOB WOJNOWSKI, SPORTS COLUMNIST,
THE *DETROIT NEWS*

Comedian Bob Newhart recalled growing up Catholic in Chicago: "The best time to go to confession was during the Notre Dame–Southern Methodist University game. You could tell the priest anything, like 'I just killed my family'…and the priest would reply, 'Well, don't do it again, my son…' and you could hear the game on the radio in the background."

—CATHOLIC NEWS SERVICE

QUOTABLE

Football doesn't build character; it exposes it.

—GARY BARNETT, NORTHWESTERN FOOTBALL COACH

Fox Sports News televised a very short report on the growing interest in God and religion among professional football and baseball players, who are praying more and thanking the Almighty more for plays and games that turn out their way.

"But if you haven't prepared and studied your playbook, prayer isn't going to help," one football player commented.

⋄

Eddie Robinson, seventy-seven, college football's oldest and winningest coach at Grambling for fifty-five years, denied rumors that he was going to resign because of a couple of losing seasons, and added: "I'm going to quit and go where—to the doctor? I go to the doctor more than anybody I know if I don't have anything to do."

⋄

Former San Diego Chargers coach Bobby Ross, keeping things in humble perspective after becoming head coach of the Detroit Lions:

"Honestly, it's players that win. I've never coached a team that had bad players and won. I still think there are three things that are very important, and I told our players this: 'There's God, there's your family, and then there's football, and they go in that order.'"

—THE *DETROIT NEWS*

"Our church had 25 guys commit to go to the Promise Keepers meeting, but then something else came up."

© Dik LaPine

For Better or Worse

"My lawyer advises me not to answer that."

© Goddard Sherman

A little boy came home from Sunday school very excited about the lesson he had read about the creation and how Eve was taken from Adam's side. A few days later, he came home from school in a seemingly distressed mood.

When his mother asked what was wrong, he replied: "My side hurts. I think I'm going to have a wife."

—VIA NORA TREECE, TRUSSVILLE, ALABAMA

The bride and the groom wrote some of the lines for their wedding ceremony. But at the wedding, the groom badly botched his lines. I coached him, very quietly, to get out the necessary words.

After the ceremony, the bride asked me if they were really married since he had so badly botched his lines.

"Yes," I told her, "as long as you never get sick."

—MSGR. CHARLES DOLLEN, *THE PRIEST*

After he was assigned to a mission church in a small town in Peru, Fr. Joseph M. Everson presided at his first wedding. The priest, who had just completed several months of Spanish studies, concluded the ceremony with these words: "Go now in peace. This marriage is finished."

—VIA LEO L. LINCK, MUSKEGON, MICHIGAN

During a premarital counseling session, a pastor asked the young groom-to-be, "When are you thinking of getting married?"

"Constantly," the young man replied.

—VIA GEORGE GOLDTRAP

Sheer joy is God's and this demands companionship.

—THOMAS AQUINAS

FMC member Al Karlstrom of Champaign, Illinois, went into a Chicago hospital for some tests and overheard these conversations among staff members:

A newly married nurse told an older floor supervisor on an elevator: "My husband is an angel."

"You are really fortunate," the supervisor replied. "Mine is still living."

One nurse asked another nurse: "Why don't they put pictures of missing husbands on beer cans?"

And another nurse described a young doctor as follows: "If he's God's gift to women, God must shop at Kmart."

"We met during the church icebreaker tonight. Will you marry us?"

© Jonny Hawkins

Last year more people applied for fishing licenses than marriage licenses. Does that tell you something?

—JIM REED, *THE FUNNY SIDE OF FISHING*

In a retirement community in the Phoenix, Arizona, area, a retired man was sitting in the kitchen eating a big breakfast his wife had prepared, and reading the morning paper.

His wife, on the other hand, was bustling around the apartment. She had both the dishwasher and the clothes dryer going, and she was pushing the vacuum cleaner.

Her husband looked up from the newspaper and said to her, "I'm proud of you."

"What did you say?" the woman shouted over the noise.

"I'm *proud* of you!" the husband repeated.

"I'm tired of you, too!" she replied.

—VIA REV. HENRY E. RILEY JR., CHESTERFIELD, VIRGINIA

"Oh, come on, sweetheart, they're just going to evaluate the first hundred days of our marriage."

© Ed Sullivan

ONE-LINERS

Many people marry for better or for worse, but not for good.

—VIA CATHERINE HALL, PITTSBURGH, PENNSYLVANIA

By all means marry; if you get a good wife, you will become happy; if you get a bad one, you will become a philosopher.

—SOCRATES

Shortly before he was married, someone asked Abraham Lincoln about his fiancée's family name.

"The Todds are very important people," Lincoln replied. "They require two *d*s at the end of their name. The Almighty is content with one."

If you think you've got problems, just remember King Solomon had over one thousand wives and concubines. Do you have any idea how many birthdays and anniversaries he had to keep straight?

—COMEDIAN ROBERT G. LEE

'Tis more blessed to give than to receive; for example, wedding presents.

—H. L. MENCKEN

If you want your spouse to listen and pay strict attention to every word you say, talk in your sleep.

—VIA REV. KARL R. KRAFT,
MANTUA, NEW JERSEY

Happy marriages begin when we marry the ones we love, and they blossom when we love the ones we marry.

—TOM MULLEN

AND IN HOLLYWOOD...

People are getting more monogamous. But there's a reluctance to get married, maybe because it seems like you're not getting married to her, you're getting married to her lawyer.

—ACTOR MATT DILLON

Men are raised with a total fear of marriage.

—KEVIN SORBO, TV'S HERCULES

© Harley L. Schwadron

FIREFIGHTER'S WEDDING FIRED UP EVERYBODY

FMC member Rev. Paul Lintern, a humorist and frequent contributor to The Joyful Noiseletter, *is associate pastor of First English Lutheran Church, Mansfield, Ohio. He tells the following story:*

Over the course of a hundred-plus weddings, I have had the opportunity to perform ceremonies in many places outside of the traditional church setting.

From exotic Captiva Island overlooking the Gulf Coast in Florida, to a gazebo on the shore of Lake Erie, to a sandbox in a friend's backyard, I have been privileged to officiate (black-and-white striped shirt with a whistle around my neck) at a wide variety of public nuptial ceremonies.

I have officiated at such "theme weddings" as western, poolside, and hippie. I even performed a wedding once at a bridal show in Wooster, Ohio, with the bridal party modeling the latest in fashion, while I modeled the latest in black clergy shirt and black suit.

But my most unusual wedding was at a fire museum last year in Mansfield, Ohio.

The firefighters' museum seemed a logical setting, since the groom was a local firefighter and the couple was on fire for each other. We gathered in a room surrounded by fire trucks and hoses, equipment and uniforms—memorabilia from a century and more of firefighting.

The groom and the groomsmen were dressed in full regalia—carefully scrubbed yellow fireproof coat and pants, with huge boots and air packs and masks, complete with helmet. The bridesmaids also wore the same yellow coats and pants, but with open-toed boots and lace bodice with a series of red bows in place of the air packs.

The bride, arriving in hook and ladder (symbolizing the way her heart was hooked by the bridegroom and that they had almost eloped), had a traditional white wedding dress, but with boots underneath the full hoop skirt and a helmet and air mask replacing the veil.

With Van Halen singing "Jump," (on CD, not live) she jumped

off the extended ladder into the antique circular (symbolizing eternal love) safety net, held by the entire wedding party. After the EMTs were called and placed the bride on a backboard, the ceremony continued.

Music included a beautifully presented harp and flute rendering of "Light My Fire," followed by a powerful oboe and guitar version of "St. Elmo's Fire." The father of the bride then sang a tearful, "Smoke Gets in Your Eyes."

I read Scripture passages about being rescued from sin and avoiding the lake of fire, then admonished the whole party to join as one department, working together to fan the flames of the Holy Spirit. The wedding party had recently joined a church that met in the firehouse and called themselves "Ladder-Day Saints."

The vows were very meaningful. They promised to love and cherish each other forever, keeping the embers glowing. They both also promised to quit smoking.

Following the ceremony, a reception was held in the museum, with guests sitting in and on the trucks. I enjoyed a meal atop a vintage 1930 pumper truck, eating smoked sausage and German potato salad.

After the reception, which the last department did not leave until early morning—just to make sure there were no flare-ups—the couple left for a honeymoon in the Smoky Mountains.

> Fires can't be made with dead embers, nor can enthusiasm be stirred by spiritless men.
>
> —STANLEY BALDWIN

"For better or worse than what?"

Simon Peter:
Personality Plus

"Some critics say that the church today is too reliant on psychology. How does that make you feel?"

© Jonny Hawkins

The following letter to Jesus and the chart from the Galilee Psychological Testing Service were composed, very much tongue-in-cheek, by Sr. Melannie Svoboda, SND, of Royal Oak, Michigan, and are used by permission.

Mr. Jesus Christ
Nazareth, Galilee, Palestine
Dear Mr. Christ:

Several weeks ago, it was requested that we give our series of psychological tests to the twelve men you were considering as possible associates in your work of ministry.

Although we are still in the process of administering and compiling the results of the tests, we thought you would be anxious to receive the test results as soon as possible.

Hence, we are enclosing the test results for Mr. Simon Bar-Jonah. His profile sheet accompanies this letter.

As you can see, Mr. Bar-Jonah's personality is characterized by a dangerous rashness, overt pride, and a lack of emotional stability that would no doubt be detrimental to you and your work. We feel also that his general physical appearance would create a bad image for your proposed organization.

Furthermore, during our research we discovered that Mr. Bar-Jonah is (to put it bluntly) an incompetent fisherman. We suspect that his lack of success in his current employment is the cause of his willingness to leave all and follow you.

Therefore, based on our testing, we highly recommend that you do *not* consider Mr. Bar-Jonah as a possible associate. We will make further recommendations regarding the fitness of the other eleven as soon as possible.

Based on the evidence we have so far, we would recommend only Mr. Judas Iscariot, who has a fine head for financial matters and would, no doubt, be a real asset to you and your organization.

Sincerely,
Galilee Psychological Testing
Service

Name: Simon Bar-Jonah   Date: April 1, 30 A.D.   Comments:

Trait (low)	1	2	3	4	5	6	7	8	9	10	Trait (high)	Comments
Inactivity Slowness	1	2	3	4	5	6	7	8	9	(10)	General Activity	
Impulsiveness	1	(2)	3	4	5	6	7	8	9	10	Restraint	He tends to act before he thinks.
Submissiveness	1	2	3	4	5	6	7	8	(9)	10	Boldness	Almost rude at times.
Dishonesty	1	2	3	(4)	5	6	7	8	9	10	Honesty	Frequently tells fish stories.
Humility	1	2	3	4	5	6	7	(8)	9	10	Pride	Always wants to be no. 1.
Introversion	1	2	3	4	5	6	7	8	(9)	10	Extroversion	
Disloyalty	1	2	3	(4)	5	6	7	8	9	10	Loyalty	He's apt to betray a friend in a pinch.
Emotional Stability	1	2	3	4	5	6	7	(8)	9	10	Emotional Instability	Easily moved to tears.
Suggestibility	(1)	2	3	4	5	6	7	8	9	10	Independent Thinker	He'd walk on water if someone told him to.
Deprived Environment	1	(2)	3	4	5	6	7	8	9	10	Enriched Environment	Suffers from a culturally deprived childhood.
Tactless	(1)	2	3	4	5	6	7	8	9	10	Tactful	Always putting his foot in his mouth.
Impractical	1	2	(3)	4	5	6	7	8	9	10	Practical	
Good Appearance	1	2	3	4	5	6	7	8	(9)	10	Poor appearance	Overweight, heavily bearded, perspires a lot.
Uneducated	1	2	(3)	4	5	6	7	8	9	10	Highly educated	

Bureaucrats, politicians, quacks, and the assorted mountebanks of the "hindering professions" are in the habit of saying everything in earnest. If we want to protect ourselves from them, we had better hear what they tell us in jest, lest the joke be on us.

—DR. THOMAS SZASZ, PROFESSOR-EMERITUS OF PSYCHIATRY, STATE UNIVERSITY OF NEW YORK, SYRACUSE

The person who looks inward usually ends up with "I" trouble.

—VIA REV. ROBERT E. HARRIS, ASHEVILLE, NORTH CAROLINA

Do something for somebody every day for which you do not get paid.

—ALBERT SCHWEITZER, M.D.

Fund-Raising Fun: Stewardship

Plans For the New Church Building As Seen By...

The youth pastor

The music director

The church secretary

The pastor

The finance committee

© Dik LaPine

A pastor for a small church was so poorly paid that he began to look for a part-time job to help support his family. He saw an ad in the newspaper for a worker at the local zoo.

He applied and was told by the zoo manager, "The black bear has always been one of our prime attractions, but he died a week ago. We want someone to come in three or four days every week, dress as a black bear, and entertain the kids."

The preacher got the job, and he made a good bear. He'd growl and run around the bear cage, and everyone thought he was a real bear.

One day he decided to climb the tree like a bear. The kids loved it. Unfortunately, the fake tree was not properly secured. It tilted over and the bear fell into the lion's den.

The lion pounced on the bear. The clawing, biting lion was too much for the bear. The preacher decided that the only way he could survive was to hug the lion as tightly as he could. He squeezed so hard that the lion could hardly breathe.

Finally, the lion shouted: "Ease up, brother! You're not the only underpaid preacher in town!"

—VIA GEORGE GOLDTRAP

"Try to avoid hitting people's heads. We're getting complaints."

WHY NOT USE COMMERCIALS IN YOUR SUNDAY SERVICE?

I believe I was the first to suggest passing out green trading stamps at church to stimulate attendance. That idea never did take hold, though I still think it would have been more effective than giving attendance pins or putting stars on charts.

Now I have another idea to help churches meet or even exceed their budgets. Advertisers pay millions to market their products on television. Why can't churches get in on this bonanza?

Why not incorporate a few brief commercials into the Sunday service? It might be a little distracting at first, but people could get used to it. They've gotten used to a lot of other things that have been incorporated into worship services.

I feel sure that church members could tolerate a few ads during the Sunday service, especially if they reasoned that it would relieve them of a good part of their obligation to support the church financially themselves.

The pastor could pause periodically during his sermon and say, "I'll be right back with my next point after these words from Frosty Fruity Flakes," or from whatever product of the day. With a little ingenuity, the church choir could even be utilized to sing little ditties to enhance the ads.

It would especially appeal to potential advertisers that they would have captive audiences in church congregations. People just couldn't get up and go to the refrigerator or to the bathroom during the commercial. They would just have to sit there and listen.

—FMC MEMBER FRED M. SEVIER, SUN CITY, ARIZONA

Rev. Steve W. Caraway, pastor of University United Methodist Church, Lake Charles, Louisiana, told his congregation: "I have good news and bad news about our pledges. The good news is: we have reached our goal. The bad news is: you still have them in your pocket.

—VIA EDWARD MORRIS, WEST ISLIP, NEW YORK

"I understand their pastor takes a hard line on tithing."

© Goddard Sherman

STEWARDSHIP MEDITATIONS

People preoccupied with making a buck usually pass the buck when it comes to their responsibility in spiritual matters.

—VIA NEWSLETTER OF WHIPPANY ROAD CHURCH OF CHRIST, WHIPPANY, NEW JERSEY

A person gives little who gives much with a frown; a person gives much who gives a little with a smile.

—VIA CATHERINE HALL, PITTSBURGH, PENNSYLVANIA

When giving to God, we are just taking our hands off what belongs to Him.

—VIA MSGR. JOSEPH P. DOOLEY,
MARTINS CREEK, PENNSYLVANIA

After unsuccessfully trying to recruit volunteers for a recent church project, our program coordinator put down the phone and said: "Not only are we couch potatoes, but we're pew potatoes, and we're raising tater tots!"

—REV. JOHN C. CRIPPS, MEMORIAL UNITED
METHODIST CHURCH, FERNANDINA BEACH, FLORIDA

Rick Moore, a member of the Crimson River Quartet in Mission Viejo, California, passed on this part of a sermon his mother heard years ago:

"Some people say they want to go to church, *but*. Or they want to give their tithe, *but*. Today, more and more people are sliding into hell on their *buts*."

❖

People whose goal is always "trim expenses, cut costs" will find their ultimate satisfaction in a piece of granite. However, those who receive life as a blessing from God take satisfaction in meeting the "never-ending" costs of a happy home or church with children and family and activity.

Homes and churches filled with life always take more upkeep than a granite gravestone. How wonderful that we, as Christians, follow Jesus. He gave His life so others could live...and threw the gravestone away.

—REV. JOHN J. BRITT, MIO (MICHIGAN)
UNITED METHODIST CHURCH

THE PASTOR AND THE GENIE

A young pastor was walking in his backyard when his toe struck what appeared to be an old lamp buried in the ground. When he picked it up, an old genie dressed in rags suddenly popped out.

The old genie was annoyed that he had been awakened. "Okay," he said, "tell me your one wish and make it quick. I want to get back into the lamp."

"I've always dreamed of this happening," the pastor said, excitedly. "Stay right here. I'll be back in a minute." Soon he returned with a map of the Middle East, unfolded it, and showed it to the genie.

"My one wish is that peace and harmony will come to this whole area, from Turkey to Egypt, from Israel to Iraq and Iran," the pastor said.

"Are you crazy?" the genie exclaimed. "Give me a break. I'm an old genie, and the Middle East has been in strife and at war for thousands of years. I just can't do it!"

The pastor thought for a while and then said, "Okay, I'll make another request. I wish that my church would be a place where everyone could live in peace, where everyone would love and respect one another, and there would no longer be any bickering, petty feuding, and quarreling."

The genie pondered the request and then said, "Do you mind if I take another look at that map?"

—REV. ROBERT M. ROSS, ST. PETER'S EPISCOPAL
CHURCH, OSTERVILLE, MARYLAND

"This is security. We have apprehended the non-tither, and we are escorting him off the premises."

© Dik LaPine

Search your parks in all your cities; you'll find no statues of committees.

—DAVID OGILVY

Thanksgiving:
An Attitude of Gratitude

© Goddard Sherman

A traveling circuit rider loved a certain brand of extremely hot Tabasco sauce. He put it on everything he ate. When he traveled, he carried a small bottle of this sauce in a bag. One Thanksgiving day the circuit rider stopped off in a small rural town, went into the local restaurant, ordered a steak for lunch, pulled out his hot sauce, poured it on the steak, said grace, and began eating.

A salesman at the next table noticed how much the pastor was enjoying his meal.

"Say, parson," said the salesman, "you seem to be really enjoying that steak."

"Why, yes, this is a very good steak," replied the minister, "but only because I added this special sauce on top."

"Could I give it a try?" asked the salesman.

"Of course," replied the minister, passing him the bottle. The salesman immediately applied a generous amount to his meal and took a bite.

"Sorry to bother you again, pastor, but I have a question," said the salesman. "In your rounds do you often preach about hell?"

"Yes, I do," replied the circuit rider. "Why do you ask?"

The salesman replied, "Well, you're the first pastor I've ever met who carried samples of it with him."

—VIA REV. DAVID M. WADE, ST. PETER EVANGELICAL
LUTHERAN CHURCH, SANTA ANA, CALIFORNIA

A new pastor, eager to make sure the church's employees would like him, called them together shortly before Thanksgiving Day approached and told them that each of them would receive a turkey. "In fact," he added, "as long as I'm around, you will always have a turkey."

—MSGR. CHARLES DOLLEN, *THE PRIEST*

THANKSGIVING THOUGHTS

We need to sing songs of gratitude, even when others find nothing to sing about.

—ELIZABETH-ANNE VANEK

Practice the attitude of gratitude.

—Norman Vincent Peale

Thanks to my friend Betty King, I can laugh at myself in times of frustration. Her question is: Do we have "gratitude" or is it a "grrrr-attitude"?

—Jean Smith, Fort Collins, Colorado

May this Thanksgiving help you to give thanks for all the turkeys in your life.

—Sr. Monique Rysavy, Owatonna, Minnesota

Sometimes we need to remind ourselves that thankfulness is indeed a virtue.

—William J. Bennett

"I've seen this in other rural parishes. He wants sanctuary."

© Ed Sullivan

Gratitude is not only the greatest of virtues, but the parent of all others.

—CICERO

Gratitude is the language of the angels.

—NOELA N. EVANS

Though I keep Thanksgiving in November, but forget that every day brings cause for giving thanks, I am at heart ungrateful.

—JOSEPH R. SWAIM

Christmas:
"God Rest Ye Merry"

"Very few people realize this, but the corner-stone of this church is actually a fruitcake given to me by Ethel Mabeline during the Christmas of '72."

© Jonny Hawkins

At Christmastime, a visiting family was driving around town looking at manger scenes. When they drove by the manger scene outside the Episcopal church, the five-year-old boy asked who the figures were.

"That is Mary, Joseph, and the baby Jesus in the manger," the mother explained.

Then they drove by a Methodist church, where the entire crèche was on display.

"Who are those guys?" the boy asked.

"Oh, those are the Three Wise Men," the father said. "They are looking for the baby Jesus."

"Well, they won't find Him there!" the boy exclaimed. "He's down at the other church!"

—REV. WARREN J. KEATING, FIRST PRESBYTERIAN
CHURCH, DERBY, KANSAS

**Pastor Stanley is visited by the ghost of
Christmas cantatas past.**

© Steve Phelps

A Sunday school class of first-graders was asked by their teacher to write their own version of the Nativity. They had the familiar cast: Joseph, the Three Wise Men, the star, and an angel propped up in the background.

Everything else was modernized. There were some bales of straw, behind which Mary was apparently in labor. Suddenly the "doctor" emerged from the "delivery room" with a big smile and exclaimed: "Congratulations, Joseph, it's a God."

—VIA REV. FELIX A. LORENZ JR., DEARBORN CHRIST-
IAN CHURCH, DEARBORN HEIGHTS, MICHIGAN

A JULY 4th ADVENT

Our Advent wreath at St. Timothy Cumberland Presbyterian Church in Bedford, Texas, has the traditional five candles, four of which have mechanical springs. The altar committee trims the candles to fit, retracts the spring mechanisms, and inserts the candles. As they burn, the spring pressure automatically pushes the candles up.

During the Advent season last year, the altar committee was unavailable to prepare the candles, and so the pastor took it upon himself to replace the old candles. Unable to find the appropriate straight candles, he chose four new tapered ones and inserted them into the spring mechanisms with the fat ends up.

A test lighting worked beautifully, and all went well for the first three Sundays in Advent. But on the fourth Sunday in Advent, midway through the pastor's sermon, the congregation was startled to hear a loud *snap* and watched one candle skyrocket all the way to the rafters, then fall to the floor.

Unruffled, the pastor continued his sermon. There was another snap, and a second candle soared into the heavens, then landed still burning. There was a mad dash by the elders to put out the burning candle and snuff out the other candles before they, too, were launched.

The Fourth Sunday in Advent turned out to look like the Fourth of July. But the pastor, amid the congregation's laughter, continued to preach in "decent and good order."

—PASTOR BARNEY HUDSON, ST. TIMOTHY CUMBER-
LAND PRESBYTERIAN CHURCH, BEDFORD, TEXAS

Question: Why was Jesus born in a stable?
Answer: Mary and Joseph were enrolled in an HMO.

—REV. DANIEL L. ENGBER, ZION LUTHERAN CHURCH,
BRISTOL, INDIANA

© Harley L. Schwadron

Bob Bayer of Westchester, California, observed that his three-year-old daughter, McCayleigh, was repeatedly watching a Barney Christmas special videotape that she had received as a present. Finally, he told her, "Honey, you shouldn't watch that tape anymore. Christmas is over."

"No, Daddy," she replied. "Christmas isn't over. Christmas is coming."

—THE *LOS ANGELES TIMES*

In preparation for Christmas, a Sunday school teacher told her children to write on small slips of paper the kind of gift the infant Jesus would like and could use. They were to drop these slips in a box near the classroom crib.

Some of the children misunderstood. Instead of the name of the gift, they put the gift itself in the box. In the box the teacher found a can of baby food, a small teddy bear, a toy truck, a tiny pair of mittens, and a disposable diaper.

At their classroom party, the children were to "show and tell" their gifts. The little girl who had given the diaper said: "Jesus was a real baby. Real babies need diapers."

—MSGR. ARTHUR TONNE,
JOKES PRIESTS CAN TELL

Becky Wuerth of Houston, Texas, tells this story:

One night in December, her five-year-old son, Trevor, was praying before bedtime. He asked God to watch over his grandmother.

"God, just lay your hands on her and help her feel better," he prayed. "Maybe you haven't been looking at her lately because she isn't feeling too well, Lord…"

After the prayer, Mrs. Wuerth explained to her son that God was watching over his grandmother and helping her to get well. "He is watching *all* of us *all* of the time, when we are doing good things and bad things," she said.

Trevor pondered this explanation for a while, then said: "I get it! When you do something bad, God waits for you to apologize to the other person and to Him. If you don't, He tells Santa."

"No, I haven't been a good boy but I now repent."

© Doc Goodwin

Nothing during the year is so impressively convincing as the vision Christmas brings of what this world would be if love became the daily practice of human beings.

—NORMAN VINCENT PEALE

RING THE BELLS

The December 1996 issue of *The Joyful Noiseletter* featured a Christmas song called "Ring the Bells" sung to the tune of "Jingle Bells." The lyrics were composed by Rev. Paul Lintern of First English Lutheran Church, Mansfield, Ohio.

Rev. Jay Hilbinger of Ebenezer Lutheran Church, Columbia, South Carolina, was inspired to compose a couple of additional verses, sung to the tune of the verses which begin "Dashing through the snow…"

Hilbinger combined his verses with the first verse composed by Lintern, and incorporated the new revised version of the song into his church's Christmas play:

Ring the bells, ring the bells!

Ring them loud and clear.

Let the countryside announce

The baby king is here.

Ring the bells, ring the bells,

Make a joyful noise,

So all of God's creation

Can sing and shout "Rejoice!"

Mary's child was born

In a stable dark as night.

The angels sang a song

Proclaiming peace and light!

Let alleluias rise,

Throughout the whole year long.

The Christ was born in Bethlehem,

And so we sing this song.

The Son of God is here,

So make a joyous sound!

We were sadly lost,

Now in Love we're found!

Church bells gladly ring,

Making spirits bright.

What fun it is to laugh and sing

This merry song tonight...

"It's the Senate Ethics Committee... they'd like a copy of your 'Good and Bad' list."

© Goddard Sherman

From the *Fort Scott (Kansas) Tribune:* "The winners for the 1997 Light Up Fort Scott Christmas lighting contest (sponsored by the Kiwanis Pioneers) have been announced. Signs will be placed in the sinners' yards during the Christmas season to recognize their efforts."

—VIA REV. ROBERT H. LAPP, FIRST PRESBYTERIAN
CHURCH, FORT SCOTT, KANSAS

CHRISTMAS GIFTS FOR THE CLERGY

The catalog of Balmy Clergy Supply, Inc. offered the following special Christmas gift suggestions for clergy, according to The Joyful Noiseletter *consulting editor Rev. David R. Francoeur of Stuart, Florida:*

The Balmy Invisible Plate Vacuum

Clergy have to attend many church meals and dinner parties in members' homes, and a significant number of clergy report they have difficulty keeping their weight down. The only way to avoid adding excess pounds was to refuse invitations, angering church members, or to select such small amounts of food that the host or hostess misinterpreted this as a criticism of the meal.

The Balmy Invisible Plate Vacuum consists of a small but powerful pump linked to a five-mil plastic bag, strapped to the pastor's back, with a long hose designed to run down the sleeve of a jacket or long-sleeve shirt. After eating a modest amount, the pastor places the end of the sleeve an inch above the plate, the vacuum pump is activated, and the contents of the plate are quickly sucked into the plastic bag. With its small size and ultra-quiet motor, the Balmy Invisible Plate Vacuum is the perfect gift for weight-conscious clergy.

Order No. 872-E Invisible Plate Vacuum...$521.32 (includes 50 bags)

Laughing Alms Basin

Everybody loves a cheerful giver, but our researchers indicate that most people do not smile nor appear to enjoy putting their offering in the plate on Sunday. In order to help your church members have a more cheerful attitude in giving on Sunday, Balmy has developed the Laughing Alms Basin. At the touch of a hand, a small digitized recording of men and women laughing joyfully is projected

from a speaker located on the bottom of the alms basin. Recent studies have shown that the regular use of this jovial soundtrack increases giving by 12-15 percent.
Order No. 965-G Laughing Alms Basin .... $167.50 (batteries not included)

© Harley L. Schwadron

FAITH'S JOURNEY

Some find the baby Jesus
    as quickly
As Shepherds of long ago,
    while others
    journey miles
To reach the manger.

—Dona Maddux Cooper, Stillwater,
Oklahoma, from *Family Ties*

Before Christmas expenses
>   begin to accrue,
My subscription with you
>   I wish to renew.
Procrastination has become
>   an art,
Which I'm taking steps
>   to break apart.
So Merry Christmas!
>   rejoice in Christ's birth!
Have a great New Year
>   with joy and mirth!

—Rev. Woody McKay, Stone Mountain, Georgia

"What did Pastor Wirt say when you told him, 'This is the day the Lord has made; rejoice and be glad in it.'?"

© Ed Sullivan

CHRISTMAS: AN ANSWER TO DEPRESSION

It wasn't so long ago that psychologists started telling us that the "holidays" are not a source of joy for everyone. Like the drunk I encountered on the subway on Christmas Eve, they've been told the Christmas season is a time we're supposed to be happy, but they can't find the way.

It does not have to be so, as I found when I was away in the service as an air force chaplain for four straight years (1955-1959). Somehow the real Christmas story came to me as I longed to be home. Wasn't it true that Mary and Joseph were away from home at the convenience of the government?

As we sang our Christmas carols amid the Joshua trees of the Mojave Desert, or listened to a four-year-old Korean orphan sing "Santa Claus Is Coming to Town" at our party for the children in postwar Korea, I got the message: "Christ can be born anywhere where there is a heart to love Him."

Against the blustery winds of Panyong Do, it was good to recall that the love of God knows no boundaries. In Him we will always be at home.

Christmas may not measure up to the warmth projected from your favorite Christmas catalog, because loneliness, alienation, and trouble are real. Some people will always have to live in their own, private war zone. Life can be hard. However, it was into that kind of world that God sent Jesus, and it was to the people of that world that the angels sang! Even without a Christmas tree, Christ can be born in our hearts today.

Let's remember the true message of Christmas: Emmanuel—
God with us!

—REV. JOHN L. WALLACE, PASTOR, THE PRESBYTERIAN
CHURCH OF SWEET HOLLOW, MELVILLE, NEW YORK.
THIS ARTICLE IS ADAPTED WITH PERMISSION FROM
THE DECEMBER 1996 ISSUE OF THE CHURCH'S
NEWSLETTER, *THE BELL RINGER*.

WORDS TO START THE NEW YEAR

Don't let yesterday take up too much of today.

—WILL ROGERS

God forgets the past; imitate Him.

—MAX LUCADO

The devil tempts us to occupy our minds with the past and the
future, so that we neglect the present.

—REV. ROBERT E. HARRIS

God cannot change the past, but He can raise the dead.

—THOMAS AQUINAS

> I may be brash
> And I may be bold
> But as long as I'm laughing
> I'll not be old!

—GEORGE GOLDTRAP, HUMORIST AT SIXTY

Acknowledgments and Permissions

⑥

Jokes and anecdotes undergo intriguing transformations as they are retold through the years. Although the editors of *The Joyful Noiseletter* diligently seek to track down the original source of a joke or anecdote, they are not always easy to discover.

When we discovered the original source of a joke, we gave due credit in this book. Otherwise, we acknowledged the person who passed on the item to *The Joyful Noiseletter*.

We are especially grateful to the gifted cartoonists who contributed to this book: Marty Bucella, Sandy Campbell, Dennis Daniel, Bill Frauhiger, Doc Goodwin, Jonny Hawkins, Dik LaPine, Steve Phelps, Dan Rosandich, Harley L. Schwadron, Goddard Sherman, Wendell W. Simons, Ed Sullivan, Andrew Toos, and M. Larry Zanco.

For being so helpful in so many ways, we also thank Rebecca Price, Lisa Bergren, Laura Barker, and Carol Bartley of Water-Brook Press; Lenore Person and Elizabeth Gold of Guideposts Books; our agent, Sara Fortenberry; and Gerrie Bridge, FMC's administrative/editorial assistant, without whose patience and good humor this book would not have been possible.

We thank the following persons, authors, and publishers for their assistance and permission to reprint the named materials:

Rev. Ron Birk, a San Marcos, Texas, goat rancher, Lutheran

pastor, humorist, and speaker, and LangMarc Publishing, San Antonio, Texas, for permission to reprint samplings from his book *St. Murphy's Commandments* (© 1997 by Ron Birk).

Rev. Denny J. Brake, a Lutheran pastor in Raleigh, North Carolina, for "Aunt Selma's Runaway Hearse."

Rev. H. Warren Casiday, pastor of Emanuel United Church of Christ, Thomasville, North Carolina, for passing along "Top Ten Reasons for Joining the Church Choir."

Dona Maddux Cooper, of Stillwater, Oklahoma for contributing several humorous poems from her book *Family Ties* (© Dona Maddux Cooper).

The *Disciple* and the Christian Board of Publication, St. Louis, Missouri, for permission to reprint "Top Ten Excuses for Not Attending Church" (© 1998).

Paulette Ducharme, OSU, retreat director at the Ursuline Residence in Waterville, Maine, and *Church World*, Maine's Catholic weekly, for permission to reprint an adaptation of "In Praise of 'Ministers of Fun'" (© Paulette Ducharme).

Rev. David R. Francoeur of Stuart, Florida, for "Christmas Gifts for the Clergy" from the catalog of *Balmy Clergy Supply, Inc.*

George and Peggy Goldtrap of Happy Talk Int'l, Ormond-by-the-Sea, Florida, for their numerous anecdotes.

Sean Gonsalves, a reporter for the *Cape Cod Times*, of Hyannis, Massachusetts, and Universal Press Syndicate, for permission to reprint his Easter column. (Dist. by Universal Press Syndicate. All rights reserved.)

Rev. Jeff Hanna, pastor of First United Methodist Church of Galion, Ohio, for permission to print "Top Ten Signs You're in a

Dry-Bones Church," and "Top Ten Ways to Tell If a Church Is Spirit-Filled."

Liz Curtis Higgs, humorist/encourager, of Louisville, Kentucky, and Thomas Nelson Publishers, Nashville, Tennessee, for permission to reprint "How Not to Move a Defiant Waterbed" and "The Case of the Missing Ice-Cream Cone" from Liz's book *Help! I'm Laughing and I Can't Get Up* (© 1998 Liz Curtis Higgs).

Rev. Jay Hilbinger of Ebenezer Lutheran Church, Columbia, South Carolina, and Rev. Paul Lintern of First English Lutheran Church, Mansfield, Ohio, for the lyrics to "Ring the Bells."

Pastor Barney Hudson of St. Timothy Cumberland Presbyterian Church, Bedford, Texas, for "A July 4th Advent."

Barb Hughes of Portland, Oregon, for her "An Ode to Sick Worshipers."

Rev. Warren Keating of First Presbyterian Church, Derby, Kansas, for his many entertaining stories. (Rev. Keating is now rejoicing in heaven.)

Clint Kelly, of Everett, Washington, for his witty advice on nurturing little ones with *How to Win Grins and Influence Little People.*

Inez E. Lawson, of Bowling Green, Missouri, for "Three Cheers for the Big, Beautiful, and Benevolent."

Rev. Paul Lintern, associate pastor of First English Lutheran Church in Mansfield, Ohio, for "Firefighter's Wedding Fired Up Everybody."

William C. McVeigh of Fountain Hills, Arizona, for "A Flood of Blessings."

Cindy H. Melancon, of Amarillo, Texas, for "Tale of the Easter Cat."

Rev. Paul Mueller, of Bowling Green, Ohio, a columnist for the *Catholic Chronicle* of Toledo, for permission to reprint excerpts from his Easter column.

Rev. J. Christy Ramsey, pastor of Ottawa (Ohio) Presbyterian Church for "Jesus and Reverend Ramsey: Comparative Ministries."

Jim Reed of Cotter, Arkansas, for several items from his books *The Funny Side of Golf* and *The Funny Side of Fishing*.

James J. Reyor Sr., of Springfield, Massachusetts, for his contribution to "Funereal Humor."

Rev. Robert M. Ross of St. Peter's Episcopal Church, Osterville, Maryland, for "The Pastor and The Genie."

Fred W. Sanford, of Schaumburg, Illinois, for permission to reprint "Top Ten Reasons Why Heaven Is Looking Good" (© 1997 Fred W. Sanford).

Fred M. Sevier of Sun City, Arizona, for "Why Not Use Commercials in Your Sunday Service?"

Charlie W. Shedd and Servant Publications of Ann Arbor, Michigan, for permission to reprint an adaptation from his book *Brush of an Angel's Wing* (© 1994 Charlie W. Shedd).

Sr. Melannie Svoboda, SND, of Royal Oak, Michigan, for permission to reprint "Simon Peter: Personality Plus."

Paul Thigpen, humor historian of Springfield, Missouri, for "Front Page Headlines" and numerous anecdotes.

Sandy Tobin, of Clearwater, Florida, for permission to reprint "Why Can't Someone Invent an 'Easter Grass Catcher'?"

Stan Toler, Mark Toler-Hollingsworth, and Albury Publishing of Tulsa, Oklahoma for permission to reprint excerpts from the Toler-Hollingsworth book *You Might Be a Preacher If...*, vol. 2 (© 1997 Albury Publishing, Tulsa, Oklahoma).

Rev. John L. Wallace, pastor of the Presbyterian Church of Sweet Hollow in Melville, New York, for permission to adapt "Christmas: An Answer to Depression" from the December 1996 issue of the church's newsletter, *The Bell Ringer*.

Tim Wildmon of American Family Radio in Tupelo, Mississippi, and Barbour Publishing, Inc., P.O. Box 719, Uhrichsville, Ohio 44683, for permission to reprint an adaptation about a nonsoccer dad from Wildmon's book *I Wonder What Noah Did with the Woodpeckers* (© 1998 Tim Wildmon).

Patty Wooten, RN, aka "Nancy Nurse," of Santa Cruz, California, author of *Compassionate Laughter: Jest for your Health*, for generously sharing several funny items.

Index of Subjects

Index of Contributors
and Resources

⑥

About the Authors

❡

Cal Samra is a former newspaper and wire-service reporter. He worked for the *New York Herald Tribune*, the *Newark Evening News*, Associated Press, the *Ann Arbor News*, and the *Battle Creek Enquirer*. He is the author of *The Joyful Christ: The Healing Power of Humor*.

Rose Samra has been involved in music and intercession ministries. She has worked for Christian education, health, and agricultural organizations.

The Samras are coauthors of the two best-selling books, *Holy Humor* and *More Holy Humor*. They live in Portage, Michigan, and have three sons: Luke, Matthew, and Paul.

If you enjoyed this book, ask for the others at your local bookstore...

Holy Humor, ISBN: 1-57856-279-1

More Holy Humor, ISBN: 1-57856-280-5

Holy Hilarity, ISBN: 1-57856-281-3

More Holy Hilarity, ISBN: 1-57856-282-1

...as well as these gift books also compiled by Cal and Rose Samra...

Mirth for the Millennium, ISBN: 1-57856-283-X

From the Mouths of Babes, ISBN: 1-57856-284-8

Rolling in the Aisles, ISBN: 1-57856-285-6

The Laughter Prescription, ISBN: 1-57856-286-4